Evening the Score

Evening the Score

Women in Music and
the Legacy of Frédérique Petrides

Jan Bell Groh

THE UNIVERSITY OF ARKANSAS PRESS
FAYETTEVILLE 1991

95 94 93 92 91   5 4 3 2 1

This book was designed by Ellen Beeler using the typeface Bembo.

The paper used in this publication meets the minimum requirements of the American National Standard for Permanence of Paper for Printed Library Materials Z39.48-1984. ∞

Library of Congress Cataloging-in-Publication Data

Groh, Jan Bell, 1936–
    Evening the score: Women in music and the legacy of Frédérique Petrides / Jan Bell Groh.
        p.   cm.
    Includes 37 issues of the newsletter Women in music, published from 1935 to 1940, with annotations.
        Includes bibliographical references and index.
        ISBN 1-55728-218-8
        1. Women musicians—Periodicals.   2. Petrides, Frédérique. 1903–1983.   3. Women musicians—Biography.   4. Conductors (Music)—Biography.   I. Women in music. 1991. II. Title.
ML82.G76 1991
780' .82—dc20   91-13807
                                                                     CIP
                                                                     MN

page iii: Young Frédérique's hand on violin. Photo by her mother, Seraphine Sebrechts Mayer. Courtesy Art Institute of Chicago.

page 1: Photo used in West Side Community Concerts brochure, 1965.

page 25: Detail from photo of Long Beach Woman's Orchestra. Courtesy Music Division, The New York Public Library.

pages 61, 99, 113: Women in Music newsletters courtesy Music Division, The New York Public Library.

All illustrations and newsletters, unless otherwise noted, are from the Petrides family collection, courtesy Avra Petrides. Many of these can also be found in the Music Division, Special Collections, of The New York Public Library.

All illustrations credited to The New York Public Library are from the Music Division, The New York Public Library for the Performing Arts, Astor, Lenox and Tilden Foundations. Used by permission.

To the nurturing women in my family—Anna, Georgia, Gwendolyn, Erma, and Marjorie—with gratitude for the love they have always given me.

And to my son Sean and his wife DeAnna, who continue to teach me about friendship and joy.

And to my husband, Jack, who has been my best friend for many years.

The history of all times, and of today especially, teaches that . . . women will be forgotten if they forget to think about themselves.

Louise Otto-Peters, 1849

I cannot ask for the right to succeed; I can ask only for the right to try on equal terms.

Edith Borroff, 1989

Contents

Illustrations

Preface

As with many others of my generation, it was in the seventies that I began to think seriously about women in the arts. Curiously, even though I am a musician, it was through the visual arts that I began my journey—in museums and galleries where I found little or no representation of the excellent and even well-known works of women artists. It is embarrassing now to realize I had not thought carefully about gender and my own profession, had not noticed earlier that the history books were truly "his story" and that I neither heard nor programmed women's music.

I began to consider the students in my classes. Where were the female trumpet majors going to direct their bands? How many women who were string majors had ever seen a woman conduct an orchestra? Other, obvious questions followed. Even with the women's movement, I realized how little progress had been made in my own profession.

Jeannie Pool addressed similar issues while preparing her keynote address for the conference Opus 3: Women in Music. Pool telephoned Frédérique Petrides and discussed these topics as part of her research on the subject of "The Women-In-Music Movement Then and Now." Petrides was not sanguine about our progress and ardently challenged women's ability to pass what we learn about ourselves from one generation to the next. She began by asking,

> What are you doing to make sure that the information you are collecting will be there, easily accessible to the next generation of women musicians? What makes you so sure that your work will have such a wide influence that the next generation of women will truly have

different circumstances, a different reality in music than this generation or any other previous generation? . . . I really don't like to talk about women in music history these days. It makes me sad, a little depressed. I think of all the years I spent thinking, writing, speaking, organizing, performing; and yet, your generation is just starting to ask the same questions to which we thought we had all of the answers.

Pool continued Petrides's challenge by stating:

> Each day as we begin our work on women in music, as musicologists, as feminists, as historians, as activists, we must ask ourselves these questions: What are we doing to make sure this information is readily accessible to the next generation of women? What are we doing to insure that each generation of women musicians need not remake the wheel?
>
> Petrides wanted to bridle . . . women with the yoke of history, to bind us with a tradition of which all of us could be proud, so that we would understand that what we did and what we do matters and that our work is part of a continuum, that our work has meaning and purpose larger than ourselves and our individual groups and communities.[1]

Feeling myself to be a part of the continuum, I felt I had no choice but to respond to their challenge; it seemed an assignment that history had given me. I owe an enormous debt, and this book is but one small payment.

It is my fervent hope that the compilation of the *Women in Music* newsletters, an account of Petrides's lifelong example, and my annotations will stimulate others to continue the work. There is much to be done.

1. Pool, 6.

Acknowledgments

I could not have completed this work without the support and help of many people. Several were instrumental, especially a nameless librarian in the music division of the New York Public Library who overheard me requesting copies of *Women in Music*. She stopped her work in order to inform me that Special Collections had just received the Petrides papers.

Barbara Garvey Jackson is a musician, editor, scholar, professor, colleague, and friend. Her interest in women's studies in music has led her to form a desktop publishing company, ClarNan Editions, in order to make available historical music by women composers. She is known for her research on the twentieth-century American black composer Florence Price and is a co-instructor of a course on women in music and art taught at the University of Arkansas. She expressed confidence in my ability to work in women's studies long before there was good reason for confidence. Her encouragement, candor, interest, and enthusiastic willingness to read and edit the manuscript was deeply appreciated.

Regretfully, I never met Frédérique Petrides. However, Avra Petrides, her daughter, spent hours telling me about her mother and father while we sat in the apartment where Peter and Riki had lived for many years. Avra's patience, help with addresses and phone numbers, frequent encouraging phone calls, introductions to many family members and friends, and general willingness to share personal papers and pictures were crucial to my completing the book. An exceptionally creative, insightful, and warm person herself, she helped make my endeavor enjoyable.

Gottfried Mayer's daughter, Christa C. Thurman, curator of the department of textiles at the Art Institute of Chicago, was responsible for choosing

Frédérique Petrides

Frédérique Petrides

On September 26, 1903, in Antwerp, Belgium, Frédérique Jeanne Elisabeth Petronella Mayer was born to Joseph Heinrich Friedrich Mayer and his wife of only a year, Seraphine Sebrechts Mayer. It was the same year that Jack London wrote *The Call of the Wild,* Marie Sklodowska Curie won a Nobel Prize in physics, Paul Gauguin and Camille Pissarro died, Orville and Wilbur Wright successfully flew a powered airplane, and the first American coast-to-coast crossing was made by automobile.

On January 12, 1983, Frédérique Mayer Petrides (Pe TREE des), professional orchestral conductor, and editor and publisher of *Women in Music,* died of heart failure in New York. During her seventy-nine years of life she witnessed many historic changes. One can chart many of these transitions by dates and maps and wars, by inventions which brought about changes in the way people lived their daily lives, and by great human creativity in literature, music, and the visual arts. Sociological changes, however, are less tangible, more subtle and sequential—not visual. For this reason one tends to be less cognizant of the impact these changes make in our lives.

For women in music, there have been many changes during the twentieth century. The reader can more fully appreciate the significance of Petrides's *Women in Music* newsletters, the main body of this book, when realizing that in 1850, a woman violinist was rare, not only in America but in Europe as well. Only the harp and piano were considered "ladylike" instruments. By the turn of the century, however, attitudes had changed, and the violin and viola had become acceptable; many women were even exploring the possibilities of playing brass, wind, percussion, and other stringed instruments.

The numbers of women instrumentalists quickly multiplied, but the opportunities for performing did not. Society generally admired amateur musical skills and talent, but performing for pay was considered improper and unbecoming for women. Many excuses were offered, but the fact remained; women were excluded from performing in their contemporary professional orchestras.

The solution was segregation. It is difficult in today's world to think of all-male or all-female musical ensembles. It was, however, a fact of life for all musicians until the World War II years. As men left for military service, women gradually were allowed to fill their positions—a process that was changing society's attitudes toward what was appropriate for women in many other occupations as well.

Petrides came to the United States in 1923. She studied, established herself as a teacher, and met and married her husband in 1931. Two years later, she founded and conducted the Orchestrette Classique (later to be renamed the Orchestrette of New York). In 1935 the first edition of *Women in Music* appeared.

Frédérique Mayer Petrides deserves recognition and praise for her many contributions and accomplishments. As conductors she and many of the women about whom she wrote—Eva Anderson, Antonia Brico, Ethel Leginska, Emma Steiner, and Ebba Sundstrom—were truly pioneers, each in her own unique manner forging a way to accomplish what she felt was her professional calling or destiny. They were frequently told there were no positions available, that their goals were impossible, or, worse, after having proved their skills and ability, were openly denied their opportunities because of gender. Their intelligence, hard-won skills, courage in not conforming to the social dictates of their time, and sheer tenacity are reasons enough to be writing about them today. These women were truly the musical protagonists in the battle for equality.

There was, however, something that set Petrides apart from her musical colleagues. In addition to her own musical achievements, she worked tirelessly to bring to the attention of the public the very real prejudices that existed (some still existing today) against women in music.[1] She published

1. It was possible for women to play the harp or piano in concert or in orchestras. The public also condoned female violinists and singers (few women were in competition with tenors and baritones). However, women who were recognized concert artists of the time—who had managers and were heavily booked—were rarely paid as well as men. Aside from performance, there were other professional avenues in music that were closed to women. It is astounding to realize that the first woman to be admitted to Juilliard as a doctoral candidate in conducting was Victoria Bond (b. 1949). Her degree was granted in 1977.

numerous articles in the major popular and trade magazines of the time, appeared on radio talk shows, lectured, and wrote letters of support to those whose courage faltered.

Her research concerning women's achievements, both past and contemporary, was extensive, and on July 1, 1935, the first edition of her newsletter *Women in Music* appeared. With the help of her husband, Peter, a newspaperman and publicist, she edited and published this newsletter until 1940. Of this endeavor she wrote:

> "Women in Music" was started in the summer of 1935 for the purpose of acquainting its readers with little known historical facts pertaining to women conductors, instrumentalists and orchestras, and, with current developments in this special field. It is sent free of charge to newspaper and magazine editors, to libraries, music schools, institutions and to individuals in New York and elsewhere. It is the first and only publication of its kind in the history of music journalism. Its circulation averages about 2500 copies per issue.

Frédérique Petrides was a professional musician, a publisher, an editor, and all the while a courageous and persistent champion of women's rights. Individuals who possess so many extraordinary qualities are forged in the circumstances of their culture and heredity. The newsletters illustrate one area of her creativity; her total persona was shaped and influenced by her experiences and, most important, her role models.

Her father, Joseph Mayer, was born in Cologne in 1858 but became a Belgian citizen in 1911. His offices were in Antwerp, where he owned and managed two factories, one that made chewing tobacco and licorice and another that produced salad oil. As a prosperous young businessman, he married a woman of whom his upper-class family approved, but who, unfortunately, remained an invalid throughout their seventeen years of married life.

After many years of searching for help, Mayer, desperate for anything that might improve his wife's circumstances, talked to his friend, Jan Blocks, a distinguished composer and head of the Royal Conservatory in Antwerp, about the possibility of hiring a musician to entertain and become a companion to his wife. Blocks suggested a colleague who was also one of his most talented pupils, Seraphine Sebrechts.[2]

---

2. Seraphine's father, Christian Sebrechts (1826–1900), was a sea captain on the White Cross Line. Her mother, Petronella Sebrechts (1834–1902), gave birth to Seraphine in 1868 in Antwerp.

Seraphine Marie Christine Sebrechts had studied with Blocks and Peter Bériot before teaching at the Royal Conservatory in Antwerp. She was a well-known concert pianist, teacher, and composer but decided to accept the position and became a part of the Mayer household, where she remained until Joseph's wife died in 1901.[3]

In 1902 Joseph, then forty-four, and Seraphine, thirty-four, were married. Seraphine is described in varying accounts as beautiful, vivacious, witty, intelligent, educated, and an accomplished pianist, composer, painter, and photographer. Joseph's family, however, did not approve of this marriage; a member of an aristocratic family did not marry women who earned their living. Consequently all ties with the Mayers—social and financial— were severed.

Frédérique was born September 26, 1903, and immediately became known as Riki, the affectionate name with which family and friends addressed her for the rest of her life. In 1970 Frédérique wrote the following account of the preceding events:

> I don't think that there had been much laughter in my Father's house up to that time [when her mother became his first wife's companion]. Father had never met anyone quite like her before—so free and so gay and soon after his wife died he asked Ser to become his wife. And thanks to this arrangement, I made my appearance in this world a year later.[4]

On October 19 of the following year, a second child, Jan,[5] was born, and the youngest brother, Gottfried,[6] was born July 28, 1907.

When Frédérique was born, her mother's closest friend and Riki's godmother, Jeanne Françoise Schenck, came to live with the Mayer family. Although the reason is not clear, Seraphine had spent most of her youth with the Schenck family, who "lived across the street." In turn, when

3. LePage (p. 191) writes that Seraphine Scbrechts (spelled Sebrechts in family journals) was "a potential candidate for the prestigious Prix de Rome had she not been a woman." The author was unable to verify this information, although many family members remember having heard that it was in fact true.

4. From the family's private collection of letters and papers.

5. Jan Christian August Heinrich Mayer was named for Jan Blocks, a Belgian composer. Blocks was his mother's teacher and his father's friend and became Jan's godfather. Jan, only a year younger than Riki, remained her closest friend until his death in 1970. For many years, he was the managing art editor of *Family Circle* magazine.

6. He was christened Gottfried Ernst Heinrich Mayer. Gottfried became a flier and remained in Germany.

Seraphine married, Jeanne Schenck made her home with Seraphine. The children called Jeanne "Godel," the name Bavarian peasant children use for their godmothers. Between nurses and Godel's care, the responsibility of the children's day-to-day care was not within the purview of the parents.

In both Jan's and Riki's accounts of their childhood, Godel emerges an important figure. Godel took the children on weekly trips to her parents' home in Antwerp, where they visited with "Grandmother and Grandfather Schenck." The "family ties" with the Schencks were to last a lifetime.

The children's education was divided between Godel and Seraphine. Godel was in charge of academics, including French and German. Seraphine supervised "the arts," which included the culinary and all that touched on music, painting, and literature. Godel taught reading and writing, but it was Seraphine who developed in the children a taste in literature.

Jan wrote of Seraphine, "Mother came off as the loveable but temperamental artist with delicate nerves, who was sensitive and lived in a perpetual but artistic disorder which Godel tried to keep tidy."

Haphazard attempts were made to raise the children in the Roman Catholic faith—the religion of both parents. All were baptized at St. George's in Antwerp, which was their only experience with the Church until a priest was sent to teach them their catechism when Riki and Jan were around seven and eight. The children dreaded the lessons, and Jan stated many years later that he was certain it was that experience which had led both him and Riki toward becoming "heathens."

Seraphine decided that all three children would become pianists, but a lack of patience on her part seemed to interfere with that scheme. Riki and Jan both chose the violin, Gottfried the cello, and Seraphine quickly taught herself viola in order to form a family quartet. Studying music and art, playing in family quartets, and frequently attending operas and concerts were all considered a part of the children's education. Their father, an art collector, surrounded them with well-chosen and excellent visual works of art; Rubens, Rembrandt, Whistler, Breughel, and Turner were specifically mentioned and remembered by the children.

Always curious, artistic, and enterprising, Seraphine began experimenting with a relatively new medium—photography. The following is Jan's account of his mother's pursuits in that field.[7]

---

7. While some of these works were destroyed, a portfolio of 261 photographs is now a permanent part of the department of photography, Chicago Art Institute. See examples of her work on pages iii, 12, and 13.

> Mother, perhaps frightened by all the fine arts father surrounded her with gave up painting entirely after marriage and took up photography. It must have been a fairly new hobby for amateurs in 1902 when she bought her English Soho Reflex. It had a focal plane shutter and looked like today's Graflex. . . . [She] started with taking color pictures . . . by the Lumiere method on glass plates. Some of her still lifes with a big flat shining copper pan, oranges and other fruit and red-headed Klara [the nurse] were masterpieces. . . . She did her own developing and printing and forever experimented with new methods. . . . The candid shot hadn't been invented yet and mother's pictures with people were all a little posed—what was then known as "genre" pictures.

From all accounts, the children, surrounded by farm animals and family pets, enjoyed an exceedingly happy, luxurious, stimulating, and secure childhood. The family journals are full of accounts of adventures while climbing trees, keeping bees, swimming, ice skating, making frequent trips to the zoo, and bicycling on the endless paths of their property.

The security of these years ended in 1914 when Germany declared war on Russia and France and invaded Belgium. World War I had a direct and immediate effect on their lives. Because the family was of German origin, they were "cut cold" by friends and eventually sold The Kitchburg, the house and area they had so loved. In August 1914 Joseph Mayer was put under house arrest because of his national origin. After a week, he was given forty-eight hours to leave the country. The family fled to Holland in a two-wheeled cart with no springs over the cobbled stones of the ancient oak-lined Roman road that led from Antwerp to the Netherlands.

From Breda, they watched the bombardment of Antwerp fifteen miles in the distance. Riki had vivid memories of this event.

> My mother played the Sixth Symphony of Beethoven (on the player piano) when Antwerp was being bombarded. She had us listen to the different instruments and explained the beautiful passages. It took me years before I could study the score and years later before I could conduct it. Even now when I hear this symphony I can hear the sound of the bombs hitting the targets and the response of our artillery trying to hit and scare the bombers away.[8]

After the war, they returned to Belgium, and in 1919 Joseph bought a house in Brussels. It was large and well furnished. The children were sent

8. LePage, 193.

to different schools; Riki to a finishing school with "international strays of many creeds and colors ranging from black princes, to white paupers. They made interesting companions."[9] It was during this time that she studied violin with Mathieu Crickboon at the Royal Conservatory in Brussels.

She idolized the work of the famous German conductor Felix Weingartner. Years later she observed, "I knew if I could learn to follow his techniques that I could be a successful conductor."[10]

In 1921 the family (including Godel) moved to Darmstadt, Germany. The children were eighteen, seventeen, and fourteen. There was nothing left of the once-considerable fortune; Joseph and Seraphine moved into a pension. In 1922, when Joseph died, the three children resided with Godel and her sister Lisl.[11] Seraphine asked a friend to share her room and remained at the pension until her death in 1930.

In 1923 it was decided that, due to the terrible economy and Riki's poor health, she should spend the summer with Godel's and Lisl's brother Ernest. He, his wife Grace, and their children Philip, Jeanne, and Georgie lived in Wilton, Connecticut, at their home called Graenest. Riki's "cousin" Jeanne (named after Godel) fondly described her arrival.

> . . . Mother met her in New York. Georgie and I were waiting at home playing near the garden when they arrived. Riki was eighteen, tall, slim, with very blonde short straight hair brushed to one side. She spoke hesitant English, and of course with Father, French, German, and Flemish. . . . We immediately asked Riki to play her violin and were enchanted as we stood in the front hall listening to a sprightly Gossec gavotte. Riki had meant to come for a summer but she settled quickly into the family and just stayed.

Riki, who made friends easily, was delighted with her new life in America. There were local dances, picnics, and parties where many artists, writers, and musicians from the area met.

Riki began studying violin in New York and eventually taught at the

9. A copy of Jan's journal can be found in the collection.

10. LePage, 193.

11. According to Jan's journal, Godel remained with Lisl until their tragic deaths in 1944. When the American air force bombed and almost eradicated Darmstadt, the two sisters, then in their seventies, fled to the nearest park. They were found alive the next morning by a nephew, who took Godel "to the country." Godel died shortly thereafter, and it became necessary for the nephew to bury her. Her sister Lisl lost her mind during that terrifying night in the park and died soon after.

Seymour School of Music. To attain some financial independence, she also began giving violin lessons and recitals in Connecticut.

In 1927 Jan immigrated and joined Riki at the Wilton Graenest home. An extraordinarily handsome young man who could play the violin, guitar, and lute, he immediately found a place in the Schenck family and the Wilton community. An excellent graphic artist, Jan soon found a good job at an advertising firm in New York.

Since conducting, rather than concert performance as a violinist, had always been Riki's goal, she soon moved to New York, where she felt there would be more opportunities to build a conducting career. She and Jan shared an apartment in Sunnyside, Long Island. While studying and teaching, Riki enrolled in a conducting class at New York University, hoping to enhance her opportunities. Finding no outlet for her skills, she began to dream of founding her own orchestra.

In 1930 Jan married Ruth Eastman, and the following year Riki married Petros (Peter) Petrides. Many years later she spoke about meeting Peter and about their relationship.

> When I first met Peter, I had never met a Greek and I suppose I thought of Greeks as wearing togas! Peter was a fine looking gentleman, a lovely person, very knowledgeable in French, Greek, and American literature, and a friend of the great writer Theodore Dreiser. I could never have done [my] work without his continuous encouragement and help. We spent countless hours researching the material for *Women in Music,* and since we had no children at that time, we financed the publication ourselves.[12]

And at the time of his death in 1978 she again paid tribute to her husband:

> Peter was such a very modest man about himself and his many accomplishments. He was born in Caratepeh (Turkey) in 1898 and lived and grew up in Constantinople. He was considered a brilliant scholar. . . . [He was a writer and Managing Editor of the Greek-American newspaper, the *National Herald* for a number of years.] He was a wonderful Publicity Man, full of creative ideas and helped many organizations. I know that without his great help I would not have been able to do my work as Conductor. He managed and did all the Publicity for the

12. LePage, 203.

"Orchestrette of New York" 1933–1944. The Carl Schurz Park concerts with an orchestra of men from the Philharmonic 1958–62 (5 years) and the West Side Orchestral Concerts 1962–1977 (15 years). . . . I am very proud of him as I have always been.[13]

After her marriage in 1931, with the total support of her husband, she founded the Orchestrette Classique. Her optimism and enthusiasm was expressed again and again in *Women in Music* and in her correspondence. In an article, "On Women Conductors," which appeared in *American Music Lover*, July 1935, she made the following statement:

> When one pauses to consider the increasing numbers of young American women who are now studying or who aspire to study in the near future, the art of directing an orchestra, one's conviction grows stronger and stronger that the day is not far distant when the sight of women conductors will no longer evoke feelings of curiosity and surprise.

In a letter to June Robert written in 1941, Petrides discussed the reasons she had organized the orchestra and stated her philosophy as a conductor.

> Back in 1935, there was no active orchestra in New York playing music written for small orchestras. A careful study of musical conditions in New York during the last 50 years showed me that the "climate" was unhealthy for big orchestras save that of the Philharmonic. Accordingly, rather than emulate the example of other musicians who started big orchestras, I chose to cultivate a field where there was no competition and for which there was a need. The fact that many other conductors emulated in the last six years my example, shows that I was right in trying to establish in New York a small orchestra (30 players). . . . Unlike other musicians I sensed the necessity of learning as much as I could regarding the practical aspect of the musical field; publicity, promotion, organization work.

She continued by speaking of the importance of these skills because they enabled her to work without relying on managers.

> I have always promised less than I could do; adverse criticism has never discouraged me. Instead I have always welcomed it. On the other hand,

---

13. Letter dated August 14, 1978, addressed to Mr. Vlavianos is in the private collection of the family.

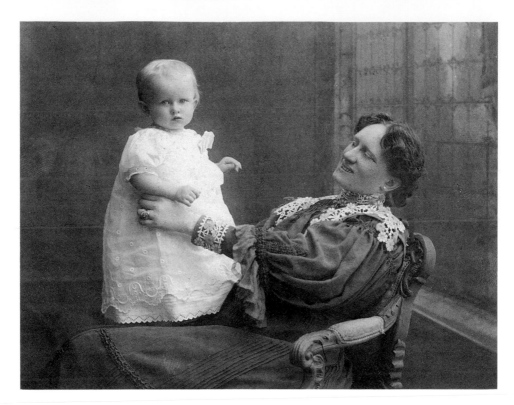

Frédérique with her mother, Seraphine Sebrechts Mayer, Antwerp, Belgium.

Photos by Seraphine Sebrechts Mayer of her young daughter Riki. Courtesy Art Institute of Chicago.

Gottfried (age 7), Godel, Jan (age 10), and Riki (age 11) in the study and playroom of The Kitchberg.

UNFINISHED
PROOF
BACHRACH

*Frédérique Petrides
in her early twenties.
Photo by Bradford Bachrach.*

Portrait Petrides used professionally as a young conductor.

*Frédérique Petrides conducting
the Orchestrette Classique.
Courtesy Music Division,
The New York Public Library.*

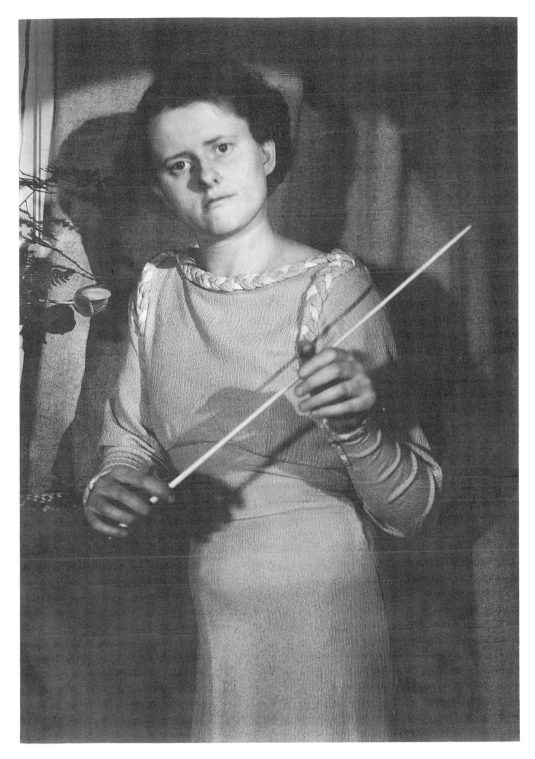

Conductor Frédérique Petrides, 1936.

From a series of photographic studies of Petrides's conducting techniques. Courtesy Music Division, The New York Public Library.

Frédérique Petrides, ca. 1962.

Professional photo of Petrides conducting without a baton, ca. 1960.

ORCHESTRETTE CLASSIQUE

FREDERIQUE PETRIDES · CONDUCTOR
190 EAST END AVE. NEW YORK · BU 8-0835

Official Orchestrette Classique letterhead.

Final arrangements for the Washington Square Park Chamber Music series are discussed by Fritz Rikko, Otto Lehmann, and Petrides, August 1957.

Petrides while visiting with her brother Gottfried in Switzerland, 1970.

Photo of Petrides taken by her daughter, Avra, New York, 1982.

Petros "Peter" Petrides in his office as managing editor of the Greek-American newspaper the National Herald, *1940.*

After a West Side concert. Courtesy, Music Division, The New York Public Library.

whenever critics wrote enthusiastically about my work, I felt obligated to myself, to my orchestra and to the public to live up to the favorable critical opinion. However, in the last analysis, I can truthfully state that I owe a lot to my policy of hiring only players who combine professional self-respect with ability and also faith in the cultural significance of our work.

Asked in 1937 to appear in Town Hall on an annual Madrigal Society concert, she responded,

Although the work of my small orchestra is conceded to be decidedly worthwhile, I believe that we owe it to ourselves, to our sex and to the standards which we have set for our performances to make our musical accomplishment entirely flawless and unquestionably brilliant before we graduate as group [*sic*] into a major concert hall.

It was precisely this dedication to excellence, her careful attention to programming, and a concern for "performance practices" that caused the critics to write favorable reviews. The Orchestrette often performed worthy but little-known baroque works with the forces for which the compositions had originally been intended. Virgil Thomson, reviewing a concert for the *New York Herald Tribune,* October 16, 1940, wrote, "To hear the music of the great eighteenth century masters . . . in such [an] appropriate acoustical frame is to begin to know something of what that music really sounded like in the ears of its makers and of its contemporary listeners."[14]

The Orchestrette also performed contemporary American music (including works by women composers) and gave a number of first performances of new works.[15] Information and comments concerning these concerts can be found in many issues of *Women in Music.* Critics continued to write excellent reviews.[16]

In 1938 Peter and Riki's daughter Avra was born.[17] With new and time-

14. Ammer, 114.

15. Always anxious to perform new and interesting works by contemporary composers, Petrides discussed her views concerning this matter in the December 1940 *Women in Music.*

16. One can find a number of these reviews reprinted in LePage.

17. Avra Petrides is an actress and playwright. In 1979 she founded The Bridge, an annual American International Music Theater Festival which brought American artists like Alan Jay Lerner and Virgil Thomson to medieval towns in the South of France, where they performed and premiered works, as well as gave master classes on all aspects of American music theater. Hundreds of lyricists, librettists, choreographers, directors, actors, and dancers from all over the world have attended.

Ms. Petrides lives in New York City, is a member of the Actor's Studio, and was the young wife in

consuming responsibilities but with the total cooperation and support of her husband, Petrides was able to continue her regular scheduled rehearsals, concerts, and editions of *Women in Music*. However, in 1939 due to the added responsibilities of a child, vol. IV, no. 8 was not published. The Petrideses had completely absorbed the financial burden of the newsletters, and by 1940 due to pressures of both finances and time, vol. V, nos. 6, 7, and 8 were not printed. Vol. VI, no. 1, December 1940 was the last issue.

Speaking of the publication, she said,[18]

> I started to edit and write *Women in Music* because I wanted the members of my Orchestrette to know that they were part of a tradition that went back to ancient Egyptian and Greek times. In 1933 people would come to hear a women's orchestra with a woman conductor, considering it a novelty, but we were really a part of something that had gone on for a long, long time. Mozart had declared that women have more talent for stringed instruments than men, a gift which he attributed to the former's greater delicacy of touch and to the easier access to their emotions.

It is important to remember that although the Orchestrette gave its last concert in 1943, this did not end Petrides's conducting career. She was a conductor for the rest of her professional life.[19] In the forties she headed the string department at the Masters School at Dobbs Ferry-on-the-Hudson, an exclusive school for wealthy young women. With the support of the head-mistress, Miss Pierce, and of Mrs. Elliott Speer, she founded an orchestra which was to become known as the Hudson Valley Symphony Orchestra.

In 1976, to further summarize her own career, she wrote to Ruth Stuber, a former member of the Orchestrette:

> As for me—since the Orchestrette Classique days I have never been without an orchestra. . . . In the late 50's I had an orchestra made out

the original Broadway production of Edward Albee's *Who's Afraid of Virginia Woolf?* She has played many other leading roles on the stage and television. In the 1970s a series of her plays was produced in New York at the Manhattan Theatre Club and other venues. Her most recent work, *Caucusus,* is slated for production in 1991. Using elements of the Prometheus legend, the plot centers around Promethia, a woman conductor who has been denied the right to her creativity and power. The dialogue is interwoven with music. Avra Petrides will act the role of Promethia.

18. LePage, 204.

19. There is a typed copy of an interview called *Madame Frédérique Petrides* in the New York Public Library collection with no other identifying information. In the interview, Petrides was asked what she planned for her future. "Conduct, conduct and conduct, . . . and I'd particularly like to conduct in Europe, especially Russia. The Russians claim many firsts but I doubt if they have a woman conductor."

of Philharmonic men—Rosenker who was assistant concertmaster in the Philharmonic was my concertmaster—in the 60's I formed my own orchestra, The Festival Symphony. Harold Kohon former concertmaster of the Baltimore Symphony was my concertmaster for 16 years.[20] For the last two seasons I have used 40 members of the American Symphony.

The concerts to which she refers were known as the Carl Schurz Park Concerts (1958–62) and the West Side Orchestral Concerts (1962–77). The organizational arrangements, fund raising, publicity, and physical arrangements for chairs, lights, and acoustical shells took endless hours. Once again, the team of Peter and Riki Petrides brought music to thousands. As to the rehearsals, Petrides had this to say:[21]

> It was necessary to be well organized because there was only limited time to rehearse. I talked very little but would get down to the business of rehearsing immediately. A woman must be better than a man if she is to conduct prestigious groups, and I made it my career always to be 100 per cent prepared and know all the scores tremendously well. I never encountered any problem conducting all-male orchestras, and we always worked well together. . . . I had very fine musicians to work with, and I enjoyed the many hours of research I did to find interesting material for the programs. I read a score the way many people read a book. I have perfect pitch and I hear the music as I read it. I read lots of music and I found many beautiful works.

In May 1979 Julia Smith, a pianist and composer who was a charter member of the Orchestrette and presiding chair of the Decade of Women committee of the National Federation of Music Clubs, informed Petrides that the organization was presenting her the Merit Award. The honor was in recognition of Petrides's efforts in behalf of women musicians. The award "represents our conductor's award, the only one given by this committee in my four years as chairman." It was in this same letter that Smith took the opportunity to express appreciation for ". . . selecting me as a

---

20. In July 1990 personal correspondence, Kohon wrote of working with Petrides. "My fondest recollection of working with Mrs. Petrides was her wonderful instinct for momentum and as a result the context was always correct. I felt about her as one feels about a military general. They both must pull, but must not push their forces. Most of the conductors don't have that marvelous instinct." Harold Kohon has recorded among other works the complete Brahms, Schumann, and most of the Dvorak Quartets and was also concertmaster for the NBC Opera Co., City Opera Co. Symphony of the Air.

21. LePage, 214, 217.

player in your first orchestra in 1932 [*sic*] and for premiering my first orchestral composition in those early days."[22]

Smith and the National Federation of Music Clubs were not alone in bestowing honors and praise on Petrides. Many other examples can be found, but perhaps one of the most succinct and fitting tributes to Petrides came from Margarita Delacorte Potoma,[23] who wrote to Jacqueline Bouvier Kennedy in 1962, characterizing Petrides as a role model for contemporary women. She contended that, in a field where women were still denied professional opportunities as conductors, Petrides's tenacity, dedication, and fine work served as an antidote against prejudice while setting an example for other talented women musicians to follow.[24]

The recognition that came late in her life may have in some respects helped compensate for the years of frustration. She did not often discuss or write of those disappointments and discouraging experiences. She saw herself as a part of a continuum and recognized that the efforts and experiences of one generation must benefit the next if we are to change the existing stereotypical attitudes of our society. Contemporary musicians have received a legacy from Frédérique Petrides; her gift was a lifetime of constant and tireless battle against discrimination.

22. See the February 1936 issue of *Women in Music,* in which Petrides wrote of Smith's work *A Little Suite.*

23. Chair of a committee for the Festival Symphony, which gave summer concerts in Riverside Park.

24. A reply to this letter came from Mr. August Heckscher, special consultant on the arts to the White House. He stated that Madame Frédérique Petrides, who had been so effective as a conductor over the past many years and who was now a conductor of the Riverside Park Concert Series, was an inspiration to all who envisaged equal professional opportunities for talented women in music.

Women in Music

The importance of Petrides's unique newsletters can be understood only when one realizes that, in many cases, her documentation is the sole historical record of the events and persons about whom she wrote.

The complete series of *Women in Music* that follows can and will stand on its own merit. However, it seemed appropriate to add the considerable number of annotations for those wishing to study the newsletters at a more than peripheral level. The newsletters are informative about their time and often poignant in light of the present, and always between the lines and below the surface there is a subtle portrait of Riki herself.

VOL. I, NO. 1, JULY 1935

Oscar Thompson (1887–1945) was editor of *Musical America* from 1936 to 1943; he was also music critic of the *Evening Post,* the *New York Times,* and the *New York Sun*. He instituted a unique course in music criticism at the Curtis Institute, for which he wrote *Practical Musical Criticism* as the text. Thompson is perhaps best known for his *International Cyclopedia of Music and Musicians*.

Rebecca Merit is later referred to as Rebecca Merritt.

Hubay and Flesch refers to Jeno Hubay (1858–1937) and Karl Flesch (1873–1944), both celebrated Hungarian violinists.

Ethel Leginska (1886–1970) was born Ethel Liggins in Hull, England, and took the name of Leginska early in her career. She became well known as a pianist, making her debut in London at the age of sixteen. In 1920 she studied composition with Ernest Bloch. She composed songs, piano and chamber music, and two operas, as well as symphonic works. She conducted in Munich, Paris, London, and Berlin before making her American debut in 1925 with the New York Symphony Orchestra. She was the first woman to appear on the podium in Carnegie Hall. Leginska founded and conducted the Boston Philharmonic Orchestra (all men except the harpist and the pianist) in 1926–27 and the Boston Woman's Symphony Orchestra (which she took on tour and later renamed Leginska's Women's Symphony Orchestra) from 1926 to 1930 and also conducted the Woman's Symphony Orchestra of Chicago (1927–28). She continued her conducting career until 1940, when she moved to Los Angeles. There she taught piano and remained musically active until her death at the age of eighty-three (Ammer, 110–11).

Henry Holden Huss (1862–1953) was an American composer, pianist, and teacher.

| NEWS, PLANS, ACTIVITIES. | # WOMEN IN MUSIC | A GOOD WILL SERVICE. |

NEW YORK CITY   JULY 1, 1935.

"STUDY CRITICISM" MUSICIANS TOLD

"An understanding of the principles and the philosophy of musical criticism as practiced in the United States is invaluable to every artist," Miss Frederique Joanne Petrides, the founder and conductor of the Orchestrette Classique, recently told the members of this unendowed but self-sustaining miniature symphony orchestra of twenty-one young, professional women musicians.

"The critic who sets out on his evening's schedule feels no responsibility toward the performing artist. His responsibility is toward his readers, toward the prestige of his newspaper and the standing of his column —aside from his major responsibility for the musical interests and standards of the community at large," Miss Petrides said. She added that "the artist or the layman who understands all this, can always be counted upon to react intelligently and fairly to a critic's opinion, especially in instances when the latter's views on the merits of a performance may be conflicting with those of the reader or of the artist affected."

Stressing the point that musical criticism to-day is an art by itself, a science with its fundamental tenets, its various taboos, ethics and technical mechanisms, she urged the player-members of the Orchestrette to read Oscar Thompson's "Practical Musical Criticism" this summer, and added that "the artist should feel duty-bound to get an authoritative understanding of 'what is what' in musical criticism in America to-day."

"Besides doing good work as an orchestra, let us also stand out as a group of professionals who believe in keeping as well informed as possible," Miss Petrides concluded.

A "WHO IS WHO" ...IF YOU DON'T MIND

The following artists constitute the membership of the Orchestrette:— VIOLINS: Hinde Barnett, concertmaster; Anne Berger-Littman; Lilli Busse; Rebecca Merit; Shirley Portnoi; Lilian Rosenfield; Zena Scherer and Elizabeth Shugart. VIOLAS: Isabella Leon and Margaret Schillinger. CELLO: Rhea Onhaus. BASS: Carolyn Potter. FLUTE: Lois Platt and Beulah Bernstein. OBOE: Lois Wann. CLARINET: Josephine La Prade and Beatrice Merlau. HORN: Helen Enser. TRUMPET: Doris Schirmeister. PIANO: Julia Smith.

A LADY CONDUCTOR
IN PEPY'S TIMES

The First of the Batonic Species

(FROM HIS DIARY)

"June 6, 1661....Called upon this morning by Lieutenant Lambert who is now made captain of the Norwich and he and I went down by water to Greenwich, in our way observing and discoursing upon the things of a ship, he telling me all I asked him, which was of good use to me. There we went and eat and drank and heard musique at the Globe and saw the simple motion that there is of *a woman with a rod in her hands keeping time to the musique while it plays,* which is simple, methinks."

HUNGARIAN ARTIST BRINGS OWN ORCHESTRA

Madame Edith Lorand, Hungarian violinist-conductor and a pupil of Hubay and Flesch, will bring her orchestra of 16 men from Europe next autumn for its first American tour. This orchestra has given more than 400 concerts abroad.

SIX CONCERTS FOR WOMAN'S SYMPHONY

The Woman's Symphony of New York will start its second season this Fall with a schedule calling for six concerts, according to announcements in the local press. Miss Antonia Brico is the conductor and Richard Copley the manager.

CALIFORNIA ORCHESTRA TO INCREASE ITS RANKS

The Long Beach (California) Orchestra,—one of the seven women's orchestras in America at present,— plans to increase its ranks to 125 players next season. There are 102 performers in the Orchestra now. Miss Eva Anderson is the conductor.

AN ENCOURAGING QUESTION

"..Why should we not have women conductors and orchestras? Why should not women play orchestral instruments?—*W. J. Henderson, N. Y. Sun, March 14, 1932.*

LEGINSKA PLANS TRIP TO AMERICA

Ethel Leginska, the internationally known pianist and conductor, expects to come back to America some time next month "to conduct symphony orchestras and opera and to once more play the piano," according to information which the "Orchestrette Classique" received last April from Mr. A. H. Handley, concert and artist manager in Boston, Mass.

In 1932, Miss Leginska's "The American Woman's Symphony Orchestra"—100 women players—gave a very successful concert at Carnegie Hall with herself as conductor and also the piano soloist. Before this activity, she led the Boston Women's Symphony Orchestra of 50 players. This group toured America twice and furnished, in addition, the music for the Lake Conneault Festival in Pennsylvania. While presiding over the Boston Women's Orchestra, Miss Leginska was called to Chicago to conduct the "Woman's Symphony",— one of the two feminine orchestras in Chicago at that time.

However, the ambitions of this remarkable artist have always made her wish to place herself, as she did with her piano playing, in actual competition with male compeers in the symphonic field. Thus, besides conducting in Paris, London, Berlin, Havana and other musical centers, she also conducted opera in New York and Boston before 1932 as well as symphony orchestras of all men, such as the People's Symphony and the Philharmonic in Boston.

Early this spring, Miss Leginska was in Florence, Italy. She was planning to spend some time in England before starting for America.

PLANS AND INTENTIONS FOR THE SEASON AHEAD

Closing its season with a major participation in the program for the Henry Holden Huss Scholarship Fund on Wednesday, June 12, at Steinway Hall, the Orchestrette Classique is at present working out plans for 1935--1936, its third season.

As in the past two seasons, the programs of the group will be made up exclusively of music written for small orchestras by Masters of all periods,—a feature in which it has been very successful. Soloists will again be drawn from the personnel, so that members of the Orchestrette may be accorded the benefits and advantages of individual appearances.

Released by the "Orchestrette Classique", 190 East End Ave., New York City.

This is the first mention of the **Fadettes,** although in subsequent issues Petrides included many articles concerning the ensemble and its founder and conductor, **Caroline B. Nichols** (1864–1939). Nichols formed the group with only six players in 1888, but it eventually became the first professional all-woman orchestra and toured the United States and Canada until 1915. The Fadette Orchestra disbanded in 1920, having played 2,025 concerts in parks and summer resorts and 3,050 concerts in vaudeville theaters. (Petrides reported a total of 6,036 in her article in *Women in Music,* Dec. 1939.) This group competed directly and successfully with men's ensembles and in fact ousted some established Boston Symphony players from their jobs. During her career, Nichols shared the podium with such well-known conductors as John Philip Sousa, Walter Damrosch, and Victor Herbert (Ammer, 105–6).

There are a number of references to **Gertrud Hrdliczka** in *Women in Music,* but beginning in 1936 the name is spelled Gertrude Herliczka.

Eva Vale Anderson (1893–1985) conducted the **Long Beach Woman's Symphony** from 1925 to 1952. She was born in Gentry County, Missouri, and graduated from the Beethoven Conservatory of Music in St. Louis. While touring with the Redpath, Chautauqua, and Lyceum Bureau as a violinist (see anecdote, *Women in Music,* Dec. 1935), she met and was coached by Howard Hanson and Thurlow Lieurance. Eventually she became the featured violinist of the Redpath circuits and while on tour played in Long Beach, California. She returned to that city in 1920 and in 1925 was asked to lead a small group of women musicians that later became the Woman's Symphony Orchestra of Long Beach. The name was eventually changed to the Women's Symphony Orchestra of Long Beach and was sponsored by the Municipal Recreation Department until 1952. This became one of the largest women's orchestras, with as many as 120 members. They published a newsletter called *Chords and Harmony.*

Herbert Whitaker, Anderson's husband and manager of the orchestra, corresponded frequently with Petrides. In a letter of January 10, 1936, he stated:

> In 10 years we've seen orchestra after orchestra come and go and the good old woman's symphony rides on stronger than ever. This layout of ours seems to be the cat's whiskers. It's not often you find a conductor and manager teamed up in the same household and where other

NEWS, FACTS, ACTIVITIES		NO CRUSADING NO PLEADING

WOMEN IN MUSIC

Vol. I. No. 2.   NEW YORK CITY   August, 1935.

CRAZY OVER HORSES, HORSES, HORSES!!

"Music is for the weakling," according to Betty Manstike, a resident of New York and firm advocate of firmness and hardihood. "It drives people to maudlin sentimentalism and brings to the surface of an individual's character softeness and tears ...," she wrote a few weeks ago in a letter which appeared in the "Sun."

"There are always ways to spend public money," stated the musicophobe, "and while it is good that a number of unemployed musicians will be put to work, it is on the other hand unfortunate that it should be spent on music. Instead of squandering our funds on music the effects of which last temporarily, I suggest that the city try to develop the public's interest in some practical outside sport, such as horseback riding. Instead of paying musicians as such, pay them as riding masters (after they have been trained) import a quantity of horses from the West and place them and the riding masters at the disposal of the public at a very nominal fee. This would help develop our citizens' hardihood, instead of constantly softening and effeminizing them," the correspondent reflected and suggested.

* * *

Have a heart, Madam, have a heart! The nearest these boys ever came to a horse was while playing "The Ride of the Walkyrie."

LASKY, STOKOWSKY AND THE BRITISHER

—Sometime around 1905, Jesse Lasky, now Vice-President of Paramount Motion Pictures, managed the Fadettes — a woman's orchestra in Boston.

—The conductor who back in 1911 forgot to appear in a concert he had agreed to lead is none else than Sir Thomas Beecham. This compelled Dame Ethel Smyth, the composer, to step in at curtain time and wield the baton for the first but not the last time in her life. — *Picture the suffragettes of those days discussing this incident!*

—Here is a quotation from a magazine article which Leopold Stokowsky wrote in 1915: *"the particular spirit that women put into music, their kind of enthusiasm, their devotion to anything they undertake, would be invaluable in the formation of symphony orchestras."*

Lady Troubadours In Medieval Days

"In the days of the troubadours and minnesingers, from about 1200 to 1450, there was a romantic female adjunct to this school of composers, especially in England, in what were called the glee-maidens. These were minstrels who wandered about the country, composing songs and singing them, sometimes to the people, sometimes to the lords and ladies in a castle, and sometimes in the courtyards of a monastery to the monks. A goat or dog was often their only guardian or escort. They usually sang their songs and played the melody on the violin or harp simultaneously."—*Louis C. Elson.*

Here and There

"Women in Music" was started last month and will be issued now and then without any cost to its readers. Its main object is to present facts and news pertaining to women conductors and women's orchestras here and abroad.

* * *

The news that Ethel Leginska intends to conduct again in America is good news. Besides being one of the few outstanding women conductors, she has done much to focus attention to woman's advent in the symphonic field.

* * *

Next to Leginska, the other artist who should head any list of internationally acclaimed women conductors is Gertrud Hrdliczka. Miss Hrdliczka is now vacationing in Europe where she intends to conduct again before coming back.

* * *

Twice last month, the National Symphony Orchestra in Washington, D. C., featured Miss Antonia Brico as its guest conductor.

* * *

A "thank you" to the Columbia University Press for mentioning "Women in Music" in a recent issue of "Pleasures of Publishing."

* * *

The Orchestrette is holding only two rehearsals this month. The group was founded in 1933 by Miss Frederique Joanne Petrides, its conductor and editor of "Women in Music." It aspires to fill in our musical life the need of a venture between chamber music and full orchestra.

CALIFORNIA CITY SPONSORS WOMEN

Long Beach, Calif., July 20.—Since the fall of 1930, the city of Long Beach has played sponsor to its local women's orchestra — thus winning for itself the distinction of being the first and only city in the world to support an undertaking of musicians on the distaff side.

The Long Beach Woman's Orchestra was organized in 1925. There are 102 experienced players in its ranks now, and plans for the coming season include the addition of about 25 more members to the personel. Its record includes more than 100 public concerts; also participation in over 1000 programs through its various ensemble units.

The group was started as a co-operative association with its member-players contributing for its maintenance. This policy was continued until the time when the City's Recreation Commission created a special tax allotment for the support of the venture. The public funds set aside for the orchestra take care of expenditures for new orchestrations, the purchase of heavy instruments, rehearsal halls, advertising and arrangements.

Miss Eva Anderson, the orchestra's conductor, has presided over the group for the last nine and a half years. This forceful and gifted artist is a graduate of the Beethoven Conservatory of Music in St. Louis. She has also studied under Dr. Howard Hanson of the Eastman School of Music.

THE NEW AND THE OLD: TWO ATTITUDES!

The sixty New York Philharmonic men who played last March under the direction of Mme. Gertrud Hrdliczka in her deservedly praised Town Hall concert, displayed such a splendid spirit of co-operation with her that the conductor could hardly find words sufficiently expressive of her appreciation. About the same time, Carmen Studer Weingartner, wife of the celebrated European composer and conductor, was to direct a rehearsal of the Vienna Philharmonic. This arrangement did not please the men in the orchestra. They aired their feelings by resorting to s a b o t a g e throughout the rehearsal — by pretending that their parts were so full of mistakes that they could not go on.

Published by the "Orchestrette Classique", 190 East End Ave., New York City.

orchestras fall down thru variance of attitude and opinion between management and leadership we can get together in short order and coordinate our objectives. Too, there is much success in having the players and public looking toward one source of authority for everyone concerned knows that when Eve speaks or acts that it is also my action and visa versa. We've got 'em coming and going.

Eva Anderson donated her library to the *Long Beach Symphony* in 1976. See *Long Beach Symphony Report,* vol. 4, March, April, May 1976. The issue carries a picture of both Anderson and the Orchestra.

Swiss-born **Carmen Studer** (1907–?) had conducted several major European orchestras before her marriage to the well-known Felix Weingartner in 1932. She met her future husband when she performed in his master class at the Conservatory of Basel (Clipping Files, NYPL).

Long Beach Woman's Orchestra, Eva Anderson conductor. Courtesy Music Division, The New York Public Library.

VOL. I, NO. 3, SEPTEMBER 1935

Thomas B. Aldrich (1836–1907) was a poet whose works frequently were set to music. He was probably best known as editor of the *Atlantic Monthly.*

Gustave A. Kerker (1857–1923) was a turn-of-the-century composer and conductor for the musical theater.

The **Musical Mutual Protective Union of New York** and the Philadelphia Musical Association were both founded in 1863 and were the earliest "protective organizations" in the United States. In 1886 this organization became the National League of Musicians and in ten years had approximately nine thousand members in 101 locals.

Dr. Charles Burney (1726–1814) was an English music historian.

See reprint of **"Outline of a Prejudice"** on pages 123–26

Ebba Violette Irene Sundstrom (1896–1963), violinist and conductor, was born in Lindsborg, Kansas, and moved with her family to Chicago when she was eighteen years old. She received music degrees from the Minneapolis School of Music and at Bush Conservatory of Music, where she eventually became an instructor. She also studied at the Salzburg, Austria, Mozarteum. She married Dr. Victor T. Nylander but continued to be known professionally as Sundstrom (See *Women in Music,* November 1935).

Although there is a detailed account of the history of musical organizations and events in Portland, *The New Grove Dictionary of American Music* (3: 614–15) makes no mention of **Murielle** or the **Portland Women's Symphony,** even though there is record of Mary Dodge organizing (but not conducting) the Portland Junior Symphony Orchestra—the first youth orchestra in the United States. In the March 1936 *Women in Music,* Petrides reported there were thirty-five players in the Portland Women's Symphony, but in the November issue of that same year Nikolai Sokoloff was reported to have encouraged the women to join the Portland Symphony Orchestra and argued against the idea of a woman's orchestra.

Petrides corresponded with the publicity manager of the Women's Symphony, Ada Albert. Albert spoke of problems she felt could be traced to jealousy. She mentioned the Portland Symphony and the Junior

NEWS, FACTS, ACTIVITIES	# WOMEN IN MUSIC	NO CRUSADING NO PLEADING

Vol. I. No. 3. *Edited by Frederique Joanne Petrides* September, 1935.

MASCULINE FACES IN FRILLS AND LACES!

The story of a man, who, appearing as Mademoiselle Olympe Zabriski in a flying trapeze act, had done such a splendid job with his masquerade as to win the heart of an unsuspecting gentleman in the audience, was told with much gusto by the late Thomas B. Aldrich.

The recollection of that story brings to mind a disclosure about men musicians in women's orchestras. It was made in 1904 by Gustave Kerker, the Musical Director of the then celebrated Casino in New York.

"The necessity of introducing men players into female organizations was demonstrated to me when I had a band at one of the London theatres", the Musical Director told a journalist. "Though the women played their best, they could not hold their own; so I had to find four or five beardless youths, who could play, dress them up as girls and mix them with the others. The experiment proved a great success musically and the audience never knew but that the entire band was composed of pretty young women."

Unfortunately for our present-day writers of droll stories for the popular magazines or the movies, the conditions outlined by Mr. Kerker no longer prevail in the feminine—symphonic or popular music—orchestral world. For instance:

In the spring of 1934 the conductor of a women's orchestra in New York was looking for that rara avis — a woodwind player. Her search was still going on when a friend recommended to her in all seriousness the hiring of a man who she knew "wouldn't mind dressing up as a woman and playing in the concert."

But the conductor had long ago read the story about Olympe Zabriski and she still remembered it with amusement. She laughed, and rejected the suggestion of putting on an act in the concert of her organization, which, by the way, happens to be the Orchestrette Classique.

THE METROPOLITAN OPERA harpists were the first women musicians to be admitted in the union. Until June, 1903, only men were eligible for membership. This rule was changed when the Musical Protective Union had been affiliated with the American Federation of Labor. The policy excluding women from membership was abandoned at the insistence of the Federation.

Did Old Venice Set The Fashion?

As far back as 1774, Venice had its ladies' orchestras. These ensembles—composed of musically trained orphans—were known under the names of the charitable institutions which were supporting and educating the artists. The Mendicanti, one of these orchestras, was heard by Dr. Burney, author of "Music in France and Italy", who wrote in the spring of that year that "it was really curious to see, as well as to hear, every part of this excellent concert performed by females, violins, tenors, bases, harpsichords and double bases. The first violin was very well played by Antonia Cubli, of Greek extraction."

Here and There

"We can't compliment you enough for *Women in Music*. It has put women musicians on a new plane and the response already noted in Southern California would more than justify your hopes. Both the *Long Beach Press Telegram* and the *Los Angeles Times* quoted therefrom on Sunday, August 18th, in their music news columns", says a letter from the Long Beach Women's Orchestra.

* * *

"Outline of a Prejudice" is the title of an article written for the fall issue of the "Musical Review" by Miss Frederique Joanne Petrides, who is now rehearsing the Orchestrette Classique for its third season of concerts.

* * *

The Chicago Women's Orchestra, Miss Ebba Sundstrom, conductor, plays on special occasions over the WJZ Radio network.

* * *

True to its motto: "All the news that's fit to print", the *N. Y. Times* of Sunday, Aug. 11, gave generous and unsolicited space to "Women in Music."

* * *

The Women's Symphony of Long Beach, Cal., Eva Anderson, Conductor, will give a concert at the San Diego Exposition on October 20. The concert will be carried over a national hook-up.

* * *

Edith Lorand, the Hungarian woman conductor, will come to this country next month and will lead her orchestra of sixteen men in Carnegie Hall on November 24.

THEY COOKED THEIR WAY TO CONCERTS

PORTLAND, OREGON, August.—"They cooked and sewed their way to concerts"—screamed the seven column headline of a story which appeared recently in the Sunday edition of the *Oregonian*. The story outlined the struggle and accomplishments of the Portland Women's Symphony Orchestra composed of thirty-five young instrumentalists under the capable leadership of Miss D'Zama Murielle.

This orchestra was founded in 1934 by Miss Murielle who studied and practiced conducting in Boston before returning to her home town. It now has sixty concerts to its credit, a record which shows that where there is a will there should also be a way.

Feeling the need of a uniform appearance for their initial debut, which took place last year at the Public Auditorium, the members of the Women's Symphony bought the necessary dress goods at so much per week and started making their own costumes. Sometime later they conceived the idea of "pop" concerts plus meals at the Public Market during the luncheon hour. The idea was put to practice immediately and the girls started cooking and serving meals to the paying guests in the audience before taking their places on the concert platform. The feat proved a success and soon the Orchestra was the talk of the town.

It is noteworthy that at the close of the season, Mr. Wilhelm van Hoogstraten, the conductor of the Portland Philharmonic, presented his baton to Miss Murielle as a token of appreciation.

Through the generosity of a prominent local woman, Miss Murielle sailed last June for Salzburg, Austria, where she is at present completing her conductorial studies thanks to a nine-week scholarship which the Music Division of the Drama League of America offered her.

DR. NIKOLAI SOKOLOFF, recently appointed to head the Federal Music Project for the Works Progress Administration, is one of the few prominent conductors in the country who admit women musicians to orchestras. The orchestras which he headed in San Francisco and Cleveland included a good representation of women musicians, according to *Equal Rights*, of Baltimore, Md.

Published by the "Orchestrette Classique", 190 East End Ave., New York City.

Symphony but noted that after the age of twenty-one there were no places for women to perform except in the Women's Symphony and wondered why the other organizations were threatened. Albert also wrote of Murielle's background (Boston to Portland) and noted that Murielle had spent much of her own money, as well as having waived a fee for conducting in order to keep the Women's Orchestra together, but had a "retiring" personality. She evidently felt this had some bearing on their funding problem. Albert's hope was that they would eventually receive financial support from women's clubs.

Petrides responded to this letter (August 1935) by suggesting that the Portland group might have something to learn from the Long Beach Women's Symphony—especially from that group's organizational skills. Petrides also stated that she had in mind a "plan" that could help all struggling women's orchestras. There is no record extant of the details of this plan.

In March 1936 Petrides discussed the Portland group's problems in a letter to Herbert Whitaker, manager of the Long Beach Women's Orchestra and husband of its conductor Eva Anderson. In this letter, she revealed that Murielle had asked to guest conduct the Orchestrette and the Long Beach group. She was denied a guest appearance on both coasts; Murielle then refused to correspond with either Petrides or Whitaker. Petrides stated that the time would come for a Federation of Women's Orchestras with the Orchestrette and the Long Beach group setting the examples of "good feeling, of mutual concern and interest in each others activity and growth. [This could be the plan she referred to earlier.] . . . You and we are in a way, doing missionary work for all women's orchestras."

Nikolai Sokoloff (1886–1965) was director of the Federal Music Project 1935–38.

Oboist Lois Wann as she appeared in 1940, courtesy of the Philadelphia Inquirer.

VOL. I, NO. 4, NOVEMBER 1935

The **Women's String Orchestra** (1896–1906) was devoted to serious music and was not paid.

French-born violinist **Camilla Urso** (1842–1902) was eight years old when she became the first woman admitted to the Paris Conservatoire. Her New York debut took place in 1852 at the age of ten. She toured the United States, Europe, Australia, and South Africa. Upon her retirement in 1895 she settled in New York, where she taught violin and helped further the activities of the Women's String Orchestra. She was an outspoken advocate of both economic and professional equality for women.

Lois Wann, born in 1912 in Monticello, Minnesota, began her musical training by studying piano at the age of six. A few years later her mother was advised to move to a warm, dry climate for her health, and San Diego, California, was the family's choice. Her father remained in Minnesota with plans to follow soon, but appendicitis brought about his sudden and early death. Wann, her sister, and her mother remained in California, where her mother eventually finished a degree and taught in the public schools.

The orchestra conductor of the San Diego High School, in need of an oboist, asked Wann's piano teacher if she had a pupil that might be able to learn to play oboe; Wann, not yet in high school, was suggested. "I loved the instrument right from the beginning but there was no one to teach me so it was necessary to teach myself. There was a flute teacher who was able to help me musically but the rest I had to figure out for myself." Eventually she was able to study several times a year with the first chair oboist from the Los Angeles Philharmonic.

After graduation from high school, she remained in San Diego as president of a local music club and played in the San Diego Symphony. She spent another two years in Los Angeles studying both piano and oboe. In 1933 Wann moved to New York and was a student at the Juilliard Institute of Musical Art. After receiving her degree in 1936, she continued as a postgraduate student earning several degrees.

She married Aaron Bodenhorn in 1942, and they had two daughters. In 1946 Wann began teaching at Juilliard and David Mannes Music School (later renamed Mannes College of Music).

Wann had a long and productive performing career. The quality of her work has been recognized by many critics and composers. In 1955, at her Town Hall recital, she premiered Darius Milhaud's *Sonatina for Oboe and Piano*—a work especially composed for her by Milhaud. She has soloed

NEWS, FACTS, ACTIVITIES	# WOMEN IN MUSIC	NO CRUSADING NO PLEADING

Vol. I. No. 4.   *Edited by Frederique Joanne Petrides*   November, 1935.

THE FIRST BATTLE OF OUR CENTURY

The members of the Women's String Orchestra — an organization started in New York in 1896—waited one, two, three years for the critics to go and cover *en masse* their concerts, which were given either at the Steinway Hall, the Waldorf or at the Mendelssohn Hall. They went on waiting, hoping, but all in vain.

Then dawned 1900—the year which found the Women's String Orchestra in a challenging mood. Its members had gotten tired of waiting for the critics. Accordingly they retaliated by inserting in their fall announcements the following challenge: "That a few critics have ignored the concerts of the Society given to audiences of 900 people, while their papers chronicle any parlor musicale, however insignificant, seems to show that there is still a pressure of prejudice against serious artistic work by women in any new line."

Shortly before the Women's Orchestra rose in protest, Camilla Urso, the famous violinist of those days, wrote to Mr. Carl V. Lachmund, the group's conductor: "....in the face of untold obstacles, you have conquered and no one rejoices over it more than I do—knowing the prejudices existing against women as orchestral players."

The challenge to the critics was not taken seriously. The String Orchestra enjoyed three more well-patronized seasons. Finally it disbanded, leaving the field to the other active orchestras of women in this country.

Throughout its existence, the Orchestra played music written only for string ensembles. It was started with 18 players who, by 1900, had been increased to thirty-eight. That its work was good is attested by the fact that among those to bestow critical praise on it were Henry T. Finck of *New York Evening Post* fame and also Mr. William J. Henderson, who, at that time was with the *N. Y. Times.*

LOIS WANN, for years the first oboist with the San Diego Symphony, will be the principal soloist at the Concert of the Orchestrette Classique on November 4 at Aeolian Hall.

Besides Miss Wann, five other members of the Orchestrette will also play solo parts. They are: Hinde Barnett, Frances Fletcher, Josephine La Prade, Virginia Payton and Shirley Portnoi.

Emma Steiner Led Over 6000 Operas

One of the very first women to wield the baton in the field of opera was Emma Steiner, the American composer and conductor who died in New York in 1929. Throughout her career, Miss Steiner conducted over six thousand performances of light and grand opera, including the "Mikado", the "Bohemian Girl" and "Mascot." On December 9, 1894, she led the famous Anton Seidl Orchestra of 80 musicians in New York in a program of her own. She was also musical director for Heinrich Conreid during an entire opera season.

Here and There

"I am all for women in orchestras. The only condition I make is that they be good enough. I have conducted orchestras (among others, the North Carolina Symphony) where it was a joy to work together with the women," writes Mr. Hans Kindler, the conductor of the National Symphony Orchestra of Washington, D. C., to *Women in Music.*

* * *

The European mail brought news from Paris about Mlle Jeannette Evrard, conductor of a women's orchestra in Paris; also news about a women's orchestra in Holland.

* * *

"Won't it be funny if, let us say, one hundred years from now, a man's orchestra with a man conductor would come to be regarded as novelty in a world so changed and reformed as to depend for its music on women conductors and women orchestral players?" writes good humoredly, Mr. G. W. Steele, 145 E. 63rd St., N. Y. C.

* * *

Concerts: Orchestrette Classique, a women's small symphony orchestra, 3rd season, Miss Frederique Joanne Petrides, conductor, Aeolian Hall, Nov. 4. — Women's Symphony, 2nd season, Miss Antonia Brico, conductor, Carnegie Hall, Nov. 12.—Edith Lorand and her orchestra, American debut, Carnegie Hall, Nov. 24.

* * *

"Women in Music" is available currently at the N. Y. Central Public Library, 42nd St. and Fifth Ave.

* * *

"More power to women, but only in music!" writes Mr. Sandor Harmati, the conductor, to the editor of this publication.

"BE LESS PERSONAL," CHICAGO URGES

Chicago, Ill.—"Women's orchestras must not merely play well; they must even strive to play better than other orchestras if they are going to be successful musical ventures," says the credo of Miss Ebba Sundstrom, conductor of the Women's Symphony Orchestra of Chicago. Another tenet of this credo is that women players, although patient, hard working and gifted, must, nevertheless, learn how to be a little less personal and emotional about their jobs.

If these days find Miss Sundstrom's Orchestra in the class of the constantly developing musical groups, the answer for such growth and increasing recognition is given by its goal for the achievement of a uniform perfection.

It is an admitted fact, indeed, that this Women's Symphony Orchestra has developed a tone and that its work has a distinct individual personality. It is also a fact that a number of its players could easily stand comparison with the first class men in any good orchestra. Despite these achievements, however, Miss Sundstrom is not fully satisfied. A uniform perfection will be possible only after some of her players will no longer be new to their instruments, she has told a newspaper interviewer.

The Women's Symphony Orchestra of Chicago was founded in 1925. It is composed of 100 players and back in 1928 had functioned for some time under the leadership of Ethel Leginska. It plays regularly during each successive season. It also goes frequently on the air, an activity which probably makes it the best known of all women's orchestras in America.

Early this summer, the Orchestra included, for the first time in its history, the work of an American woman composer. The composer to be thus honored was Eleanor Everest Freer. Her "Spanish Ballet Fantasy" was played before an audience of 20,000 at the Grant Park Shell.

ETHEL LEGINSKA, the internationally known pianist, conductor and composer, whose plans to come back to America, were, for the first time, announced in the July issue of *"Women in Music,"* is to conduct "Gale"—her own opera—which will be given at the Chicago Civic Opera House the last week of November. "Gale" will be rendered in one act and will take about one hour's time.

Published by the "Orchestrette Classique", 190 East End Ave., New York City.

with the New Friends of Music Chamber Orchestra, Bach Circle, Adolf Busch Chamber Players, the Budapest String Quartet, and the Juilliard String Quartet, among others. She also was first oboist with the Pittsburgh, St. Louis, Chautauqua, and San Diego symphony orchestras, and Les Concerts Symphoniques of Montreal, Canada. She was a performing artist and faculty member with the Aspen Music Festival and School from 1951 through 1957. At seventy-eight, she continues a heavy teaching schedule at Juilliard as well as maintaining a private studio.

Wann's memories of Petrides cover many years. She not only played in the original Orchestrette but also in the West Side Concert Series. "It was always a joy—her programs were always so interesting and she had such a special way of bringing out the music." (Telephone interview with the author, September 1, 1990.)

Emma Steiner (c.1852–1929) led a fascinating and diverse life but there is little written about her. Steiner began composing when quite young, and her first conducting jobs were with Gilbert and Sullivan companies. In 1897, while continuing to compose, she conducted forty members of the New York Metropolitan Orchestra in a series of concerts. After two serious illnesses, doctors ordered rest and she promptly went to Nome, Alaska. There she bought provisions and tools, put them on her back and set out for the tin mines one hundred miles northwest of Nome. As the first white woman to work in that area, she was credited with having discovered important deposits. After ten years of this adventurous lifestyle, she returned to New York and in 1921 gave a concert of her own works called Harmony and Discord. Toward the end of her life she decided to found a Home for Aged and Infirm Musicians. There was a Golden Jubilee concert at the Metropolitan in 1925 to recognize and honor Steiner with proceeds donated to this project. At that time Steiner had conducted more than six thousand performances of more than fifty different operas and operettas. Petrides wrote about Steiner in *Women in Music* (January, February 1937, January 1938). She also discussed her life and contributions in a 1938 NBC radio show called "Let's Talk it Over."

> There is some confusion over Steiner's dates. Ammer (pp. 167–68), who has put together as complete an account as can be found of her career as a composer and conductor as well as her ten years in Alaska, suggests she was born in Baltimore, Maryland, in 1852 but also mentions the many discrepancies found in journals and newspapers. Petrides wrote that she was born in 1867 (*Women in Music,* February 1937). The *Herald*

Tribune, when writing her obituary, determined her death to be February 28, 1928, noting she was seventy-three years old.

Hans Kindler (1892–1949) was director of the National Symphony Orchestra for seventeen years and programmed works by women composers.

Jeanette Evrard is discussed in the November 1936 and September 1937 issues under the name Jane Evrard.

Sandor Harmati (1892–1936) was a well-known violinist, conductor, and composer of the times (best remembered for the song "The Bluebird of Happiness"). In correspondence he referred to *Women in Music* as Petrides's "amusing and valuable little publication."

The **Woman's Symphony of Chicago** was also called the **Chicago Woman's Symphony Orchestra.** It was eventually a large orchestra of one hundred players and was founded in 1925 by Elena Moneak with the help of other musicians such as clarinetist Lillian Poenisch (*Women in Music,* September 1937). Moneak was the ensemble's first conductor. In a brochure describing the organization, Miss Moneak's picture was featured and an article titled "An Achievement" stated:

> For many years Miss Moneak, who has gained an enviable reputation for herself as a concert violinist was engaged as musical director and conductor of one of the large theatres of this city, having under her baton men. It was during that time that this energetic wide awake young woman conceived the idea and then set out upon the colossal task of organizing the Chicago Woman's Symphony Orchestra, thus creating not only an opportunity for women to play in orchestras under dignified circumstances, but also to establish an outlet as well as a means of livelihood in a field hitherto barred to women.

Moneak wrote to Petrides describing those early years and remarked that she conducted the ensemble for almost four years before "the inevitable" happened. She felt that, in the process of growth and progress, there had been "friction" that became more than she could tolerate—especially since she had not been paid for her services. She told Petrides that she had resigned but that she felt the Woman's Symphony was doing quite nicely at the time she wrote (1937). There is a discrepancy, however, since the program for the 1927–28 (second) season lists Ethel Leginska as the conductor and Ebba Sundstrom as assistant conductor. The program notes state that "the second season of the Womans Symphony Orchestra of Chicago is marked by the engagement of Ethel Leginska as conductor." Another curious turn in the written history of this group is that in an article, "The Tenth Anniversary of the Woman's Symphony Orchestra of Chicago," which was included in their program notes, it is stated that the group was "founded in 1925 by a group of young women, Lillian Poenisch, Lois C. Bichl, and Adeline E. Schmidt," with no mention of Moneak. The same summary also states that Mme. Leginska was succeeded in 1929 by Ebba Sundstrom, who ". . . has held the baton with distinguished success. The membership is entirely feminine including players of all the more unusual instruments, such as double-bass, French horn, tuba, and tympani."

Ebba Sundstrom remained as conductor with Gladys Welge as the assistant conductor until 1937. During her tenure she programmed music by women composers as well as the standard repertoire.

Petrides corresponded with Sundstrom and Claire Page, the orchestra's business manager. Page wrote of Sundstrom's 1937 travel plans (Salzburg and Bayreuth Festivals) and also reported in 1936 that the orchestra was operating without a deficit—a significant fact in the life of any orchestra in 1936 (or now, for that matter). (See *Women in Music,* June 1937 concerning the support of local women's clubs.)

Izler Solomon (1910–87) took the podium in 1939 and, according to *Time,* October 30 1939, he began by firing six of the players and "cowed" five into resigning. Solomon had been hired by Mrs. Royden J. Keith, socialite and president of the orchestra's board of directors. If women's musical activities were reported at all in the major tabloids of the time, the following excerpt from the *Time* article is typical of the approach taken.

> Chicago wits nicknamed the orchestra "Solomon and his Wives," or "87 Girls and a Man." But when Solomon led his black-dressed musical harem through Mendelssohn's *Italian Symphony,* Chicago critics agreed that a man was just what The Woman's Symphony had needed all along.
>
> In the audience, among the mink-coated sponsors, there were still some stormy echoes. President Mrs. Royden Keith, who had got Solomon his job, had resigned . . . So ex-President Keith had to sit

downstairs in an ordinary orchestra seat, while platinum-blond Acting-President Mrs. James George Shakman (whose Pabst Brewery money helps feed the orchestra's kitty) basked in a box. Beamed she: "We are all working in perfect harmony. The girls are such fine musicians, they should be supported. Why, think of all the money that is spent in night clubs! . . ."

Arthur P. Schmidt, president of Arthur P. Schmidt Co., a Boston music publisher, wrote Petrides after reading this issue and suggested that Sundstrom had previously played Mrs. H. H. Beach's Gaelic Symphony.

Eleanor Warner Everest Freer (1864–1942) began her career as a singer. Her father, Cornelius Everest, an organist in Philadelphia, and her mother, Ellen Clark, a singer, were her first teachers. In 1883 she went to Paris and studied the Marchesi method of teaching voice with Madame Mathilde Marchesi. She married Archibald Freer of Chicago in 1891, and the young couple went to Leipzig for seven years, where he studied medicine and she continued her music studies. Their only child, Eleanor, was born during this time. Freer began to compose in 1902. While writing numerous chamber and piano works, her compositions were mainly vocal. She wrote many art songs—mostly settings of English poems.

One assumes this to be **Luisa Tetrazini** although her sister Eva was also well known at the time.

Herliczka also wrote Petrides that, because the orchestra members knew she always conducted from memory, they decided to test her by hiding her score just before the concert (September 1935).

Teresa Carreño (1853–1917) was born in Venezuela and made her New York debut when she was only eight years old. She studied with Gottschalk and Rubinstein and enjoyed a successful career in the United States and Europe. She also studied voice and eventually organized an opera company in Venezuela, where she both sang and served as its conductor. Petrides discussed this aspect of her career in *Women in Music,* February 1940.

In New York City in February 1990, Pamela Ross opened in a one-woman show at the INTAR Theatre. The musical, directed by Gene Frankel, was based on the life of Carreño.

Henry T. Finck (1854–1926) was a music critic and author of several books about music, including *Musical Laughs: Tittle-tattle, and Anecdotes, Mostly Humorous, about Musical Celebrities* (1924; reprint, New York: Gale Research, 1971).

Dame Ethel Smyth (1858–1944) was a well-known English composer. Her opera *Der Wald* was the first opera composed by a woman to be performed at the Metropolitan Opera (1902), although she is perhaps best known for her opera *The Wreckers.* She frequently conducted her own works and made numerous appearances with the London and BBC orchestras. Smyth was a militant leader for woman suffrage in England and was imprisoned for two months as a result of this involvement. She composed "March of the Women," which became the battle song of the Women's Social and Political Union, of which she was an avid supporter. It was reported that she conducted fellow suffragettes in this march with a toothbrush from her cell window. Smyth was the author of a number of books and essays and was made Dame of the British Empire in 1922.

Pauline Viardot-Garcia (1821–1910) was a celebrated mezzo soprano and composer.

NO NEWS
JUST STORIES

WOMEN IN MUSIC

HOLIDAY
GREETINGS

Vol. I. No. 5.   *Edited by Frederique Joanne Petrides*   December, 1935

AMONG THE pilgrims to a Viennese shrine where a piano used by Beethoven is preserved, was an American girl one day who walked airily to the instrument and began playing a careless tune. Then, turning to the custodian she said: "I suppose you have many visitors here every year? —"A great many" was the reply.— "Many famous people, no doubt? — "Yes: Paderewski came recently: — "I suppose, of course, he played on the piano", said the girl, her fingers still on the keys. — "No" said the verger, "he did not consider himself worthy."

* * *

ADELINE PATTI, the famous singer was very vain. In a contract she once made with a manager, she asked that a clause be inserted to the effect that her name should appear on all posters "in a separate line of large letters . . at least, one third larger than those employed for the announcement of any artiste."

* * *

TETRAZINI, the famous prima donna used to occupy rather humble rooms while touring in her young days. One day, she was thanking a landlady who had been more considerate and kinder than most. The good lady looked up to Tetrazini and said with benign condensation: "That's all right, my dear.. I am always kind to theatrical folks, for I never know what my own children may come to."

* * *

GERTRUD HRDLICZKA, the conductor, recently had all Paris at her feet. "While rehearsing a radio concert," she writes, "being comparatively small, I stood on a large telephone book of the City of Paris. In other words, the French Metropolis was lying at my feet!!"

* * *

REFERRING TO an early impersonation of the Egyptian "Aida" by an American prima donna whose voice at that time was not as warm as it became later, Mr. W. J. Henderson wrote: "Icicles hung on the palms and there was skating on the Nile."

* * *

TERESA CARRENO was one of the greatest pianists of her day, but as for marriage — well did not James Hunecker, the famous critic and writer, write that at her first New York recital she played the second concerto of her 3rd husband?

WHEN MENDELSSOHN'S "Saint Paul" had its first hearing in Liverpool, in 1836, the Journal of that city remarked: "Madame Carradori had little to do and that little she did carelessly. She was the nominal, and Mrs. Wood the actual prima donna of the festival. Her inattention was remarkable. One half of the time she was forcing Mrs. Knyvett to chat with her, and they diversified this by the pleasing amusement of comparing the size of their respective hands and examining the texture of their cambric handkerchiefs! This during the performance of a sacred oratorio, was too bad"

"Women in Music" believes that the public should be invited to smile occasionally over the human and humorous side of musicians; hence this holiday issue with anecdotes only.

With the exception of the stories on women conductors and that about Dame Smyth, the rest of the material for this number has been borrowed from Finck's "Musical Laughs".

Incidentally, it was Mr. Finck who wrote that the trouble with musicians is that they "take themselves and their art altogether too seriously". He thought they would be better off if they didn't!

ETHEL SMYTH, the militant English composer confided a few years ago: "In 1911, I contrived somehow or other to give a Smyth concert which in the end I had to conduct myself (never having conducted before, let alone a chorus) because Thomas Beecham, who had very kindly promised to do it for me, unfortunately forgot all about it, and when the critical moment came was travelling on the Continent, no one knew where."

* * *

WOMEN PIANISTS were not among the artists whom Brahms could tolerate. One evening when seated by request next to Teresa Carreno, he commenced a diatribe on his favorite theme: "I hoped to make my two piano concertos prohibitive for women players, and thought I had succeeded, but" — here he gave a desperate grown — "they will play them."

An embarrassing silence fell upon the company, but Carreno with her ready tact, took the dilemma by the horns and said: "But my dear Maestro, here I sit overwhelmed with mortification! — "My dear child", Brahms replied, "you don't for a moment suppose that this remark was directed at you; I always look upon you as a man pianist!"

EVA ANDERSON, the conductor of the Long Beach Women's Orchestra writes: "Some years ago a lyceum company, under Redpath booking, lost their solo violinist and I was dispatched at once to fill the gap temporarily. In my position I found that among other skits the 'Toreador Song' from Carmen had a place on the program with all hands joining in the vocal chorus. Now, singing was never my forte, but if singing was called for then we would sing and I applied myself lustily to its performance. The company manager was the essence of tact and diplomacy, for he approached me before the next appearance and suggested: "Now we feel that we should have a little more instrumental support in the 'Toreador Song' and if you don't mind would you just as soon play and not sing?"

* * *

AN AMERICAN lady called on a famous singing teacher in Paris and said: "I guess I want two lessons" — "And pray why two lessons?"— "I guess because it's plural" answered the American. She was coming back to her country to say that she had had lessons with Madame Viardot-Garcia, the great prima donna and teacher.

* * *

MAUD POWELL, the famous violinist, stopped in the course of one of her artistic tours, at a new hotel in Texas. She was very hungry when she went down to dinner, but everything she ordered was so badly cooked that she could not eat it. Finally, she got up in despair. In the elevator, unable to repress her feelings, she said to the boy who ran it: "This is positively the worst hotel I have been in." — "Yes, ma'am" he replied, "that's what everybody says."

* * *

JENNY LIND, didn't seem to care very much for excessive applause. After her second appearance in Vienna in "Norma" she wrote: "Was called so many times before the curtain that I was quite exhausted. Bah! I do not like it. Everything should be done in moderation; otherwise is not pleasing."

* * *

TWO YEARS AGO, the conductor of the Orchestrette Classique gave an audition to an ambitious young player, who wanted to join her group of women musicians.

"I like your technique and enthusiasm, but I can't take you in the Orchestrette. I notice that you are playing out of tune" the applicant was told after she had finished.

"But, Miss Petrides, since you like my technique and enthusiasm, why let a little thing like playing out of tune stand in my way?" was the naive answer.

Published by the "Orchestrette Classique", 190 East End Ave., New York City.

VOL. I, NO. 5, DECEMBER 1935.

In 1885 **Maud Powell** (1867–1920) made her European debut with the Berlin Philharmonic under Joseph Joachim and her American debut with the New York Philharmonic under Theodore Thomas. At the World's Columbian Exposition (1893) she delivered a paper, "Women and the Violin," to the Women's Musical Congress. Powell was the first American woman to form and lead a professional string quartet (1894). She also formed a trio in which her sister Ann Mukle Ford played; this group toured the United States. Powell was the first violinist to record for the Victor Talking Machine Co. and was considered by many to be one of America's greatest violinists. In "Mixed Orchestras in Earlier Days" (*Women in Music,* October 15, 1937), Petrides makes reference to an article written by Powell in 1909 concerning the first attempts at "mixed orchestras."

Jenny Lind (1820–1887), a Swedish soprano, was known in the United States as "the Swedish nightingale." While touring this country, she was managed by P. T. Barnum.

Conductor Gertrude Herliczka. Courtesy Music Division, The New York Public Library.

VOL. I, NO. 6, FEBRUARY 1936

Petrides submitted an article to Peter Reed, editor of *The American Music Lover* on **Caroline B. Nichols**. He wrote September 20, 1937, that he would agree to consider publishing the article because of his admiration for Petrides but was generally unenthusiastic about the subject and suggested that she might try elsewhere.

Julia Smith (1911–89) was born in Texas but, after completing a bachelor of arts degree from North Texas State, moved to New York, where she studied with Lonny Epstein (frequent soloist with the Orchestrette) and Carl Friedberg at Juilliard. It was while at New York University working on her master's degree that she met Petrides in a conducting class. They performed together and became lifelong friends. Smith was the pianist in the Orchestrette when it was first formed, and Petrides performed and premiered a number of Smith's compositions. The specific work mentioned here, *A Little Suite Based on American Folk-Tunes,* was later revised and renamed *American Dance Suite*. Smith wrote a number of operas as well as chamber, orchestral, and vocal works. She was also the author of several books. In 1979, as chair of the Decade of Women committee of the National Federation of Music Clubs, she presented a Merit Award to Petrides in recognition of her efforts on the behalf of women musicians.

Antonia Brico (1902–89), founder and conductor of the **New York Women's Symphony**, was born in Rotterdam, Netherlands, but came to the States when she was six and graduated from the University of California, Berkeley in 1923. She spent five years (1925–30) at the Berlin school of conducting and made her debut in 1930 with the Berlin Philharmonic. In 1933 Brico returned to the States and made many guest appearances with major orchestras. Brico founded and conducted the New York Women's Symphony in 1935. After the demise of this ensemble, Brico moved in 1942 to Denver, Colorado, where she taught and eventually founded the Denver Businessmen's Orchestra, which later was renamed the Brico Symphony. In 1973 a film, *Antonia: A Portrait of the Woman,* was made of her life, documenting the difficulties she had encountered because of her gender. The film sparked a new interest, and although Brico was then in her seventies, she rose to the challenge and began a new career.

Unlike Petrides's group, Brico's New York Women's Symphony was large (eighty-six players). It followed its debut on February 18, 1935, in Carnegie Hall with two more concerts and in 1935–36 played a full season at Carnegie Hall. The ensemble continued to be successful (*Women in Music,* April 1938), and Brico felt they had proved that women could be as

| NEWS, FACTS, ACTIVITIES |

WOMEN IN MUSIC

| NO CRUSADING NO PLEADING |

Vol. I. No. 6. *Edited by Frederique Joanne Petrides* FEBRUARY, 1936

IT WAS A VERY HARD TEST FOR CHIVALRY!

"The Boston Symphony Orchestra is in danger of serious dissension and all because women have invaded the musical field. The Symphony players are nearly all Germans, and when not playing at Symphony Hall are mostly engaged in giving instruction", said a story which appeared in the "New York Herald" of April 19, 1902, and which is reprinted here in full.

"Many of their pupils are young women, about twenty of the latter at the present time being members of the Fadette Women's Orchestra. This organization did not attract much attention in Boston until a few weeks ago when it appeared at Keith's Theatre and made a decided hit.

"In fact, it drew such audiences that the management decided to engage it for a few weeks during the summer season. This meant that the Symphony players were to be supplanted by women, the Symphony players having been for several years a summer attraction at Keith's.

"Now the players who had no part in teaching the women are blaming the men who made them so proficient that they have been able to get the "snap" musical engagement of the summer, while the Symphony players are making their contracts with summer hotels."

The Women's Orchestra discussed in the preceding lines, was started by Caroline B. Nichols, a Boston violinist who said in 1910: "I don't believe in rules. The minute you make them the girls try to find a way to get around them and that makes them sneaky."

Miss Nichol's group was active up to the end of the World War.

A LITTLE SUITE based on American folk tunes and written by Julia Smith, a Juilliard fellowship pupil of Rubin Goldmark, will have its first performance at the concert of the Orchestrette Classique, on Monday evening, February 10, at Aeolian Hall. The program for this concert features Miss Betty Paret as soloist in Haendel's Harp Concerto No. 6 (first performance with an orchestra in America;) also, Lois Wann, oboe soloist in Bach's Sinfonia to Church Cantata No. 12. (Miss Smith has been a member of the Orchestrette since 1933.)

The Virginian Reel And Father George

Washington's birthday this month brings to mind Nellie Custis, his adopted daughter, who was one of the first American women to start giving musicales in this country. Started after the Revolution, her concerts were held in celebration of each successive birthday of her illustrious stepfather, who, by the way, seems to have been quite fond of music. They comprised, year after year, the same few songs and pieces. Their most important feature, however, was the Virginian reel, which Father George kept up once "for three hours and then called it a pretty little frisk."

Here and There

Mr. John W. Teed, the music critic on the "Long Beach, California, Sun," likes "Women in Music." He says so in a letter in which he also praises the achievements of Miss Eva Anderson and her Long Beach Women's Symphony.

* * *

A recent Associated Press story said that the Chicago Women's Symphony is described "as the only well-established professional orchestra" of its kind in the world.

* * *

The period between 1870 and 1900 in its relation to women musicians in America is the subject of an article written by Frederique Joanne Petrides, conductor of the Orchestrette Classique, for the current issue of the "American Music Lover".

* * *

The New York Women's Symphony is celebrating its first anniversary this month.

* * *

The following publications have quoted recently from or have commented on the contents of "Women in Music": "New York Sun", "N. Y. Evening Post", "San Diego, (California) Union", "Music and Musicians," Seattle, Washington, "Equal Rights", the feminine weekly in Baltimore, Md., "Musical Review," Brooklyn, N. Y. Also "Woman's Work and Education," which stated that this page's "interesting news items would be excellent for the counselor's bulletin board." Incidentally, 'Woman's Work' is the organ of the Institute of Women's Professional Relations.

LOS ANGELES GROUP, A TESTED VETERAN

LOS ANGELES.—A forty-two year record of continuous existence has just been established by the Los Angeles Women's Symphony Orchestra, the group which was started in the "gilded nineties" and is now hailed as the veteran among all organizations of its kind in the world.

Writing about one of this Orchestra's first rehearsals, the "Los Angeles Examiner" stated in its issue of November 29, 1893: "Yesterday morning, a troop of young women came down the steps of Lawrence Hall on Fifth Street with a peculiar rapt and uplifted expression on each fine face. In their hands they carried music and also musical instruments, trombones, cornets, violins, cellos, which for the last two hours had been filling the neighbors of Fifth Street with notable music. These young women composed the Women's Orchestra which has been organized under the efficient leadership of Professor Harley Hamilton."

Organized in order to afford its members the "opportunity for the study of music written for symphony orchestras", the Los Angeles women's ensemble has had no definite schedule throughout its long existence but has given from three to eight concerts each year. It was started with 25 members and is now composed of 70 players under the leadership of Mr. D. C. Cianfoni, former conductor of the Orange County Symphony of Santa Anne, California. It has just given its second concert of the season and will play again on the evening of March 18, at the Trinity Auditorium.

NEW YORK.—Under the heading, "Make Way for the Ladies", a recent 'Musical America' editorial, commented favorably on the merits of women as conductors and orchestral players and deplored the non-inclusion of instrumentalists on the distaff side in symphonies.

"Our conductors", this editorial added, "will find in the ranks of women players fine artists, who will co-operate with male members, if given the opportunity. Artistically, we believe that orchestras made up of both sexes may in the future reveal tonal qualities as yet unknown and unsuspected."

Published by the "Orchestrette Classique", 190 East End Ave., New York City.

competent as men. In 1938 Brico admitted ten men to the orchestra and renamed it the Brico Symphony (*Women in Music,* January 1939). In spite of good reviews, this ensemble did not survive. In the summer of 1938 Brico conducted the New York Philharmonic at Lewisohn Stadium (*Women in Music,* September 1938).

Petrides had felt it unwise to compete with large established orchestras and therefore founded a smaller chamber orchestra. She faithfully recorded Brico's activities and gave her justified praise. However, she noted that the New York Women's Symphony had programmed a transcription by J. S. Bach for four harpsichords of a concerto that Vivaldi wrote for four violins and that the Orchestrette would be playing the same composition in its original form (*Women in Music,* February 1938). It is also interesting that Brico and Petrides shared some of the same personnel. Lois Wann, for example, soloed with the New York Women's Symphony (*Women in Music,* December 1937) while still playing regularly with the Orchestrette.

It is curious that there is no record of correspondence with Brico in Petrides's papers since these two women were so active at the same time with many of the same goals.

Harley Hamilton (1861–1933) was concertmaster of the Los Angeles Philharmonic before he became the conductor of the **Woman's Orchestra of Los Angeles.** He was known as a program builder and put these talents to work in 1893 by forming the Woman's Symphony. He conducted this group for twenty seasons. In its inception, many of its members were amateur musicians, but the organization quickly grew to a larger (approximately seventy-five musicians) and very stable professional organization. The situation was unusual in that the founder and conductor of the Women's Orchestra was also the conductor of the same city's large and established municipal orchestra.

Petrides also wrote of **D. Cesar Cianfoni**, who followed Hamilton as conductor. Cianfoni was a native of Italy who became an American citizen. He began his career in Philadelphia, Pa., in 1906 but moved to the Pacific Coast, where he became "an outstanding figure in musical activities not only because of his striking ability as conductor, but also because of his marked talent as composer." He was a member of the Italian Society of Composers and Authors of Rome (Program for Woman's Symphony Orchestra, 1935–36 season).

Caroline B. Nichols.
Courtesy Music Division,
The New York Public Library.

The Fadette Women's Orchestra, Caroline B. Nichols, conductor. Courtesy
Music Division, The New York Public Library

VOL. I, NO. 7, MARCH 1936

Sir Henry Wood (1869–1944) was born in London of musical parents. He studied at the Royal Academy, and in 1923 he was appointed to the faculty. Wood introduced the contemporary music of his time to London audiences and was one of the first conductors to make recordings. One of his many recordings for Columbia includes Bach's Harpsichord Concerto No. 1 with Harriet Cohen as the soloist. It is now a tradition to play his arrangement of *Fantasia on English Sea Songs* on the final night of the Prom Concerts each year. Wood ". . . adopted the Continental low pitch (A:435), and introduced women into the orchestra. . . . [He] did more than anyone to pave the way for the later excellence of London as an international music centre" (Holmes, 723–25).

Marie Wilson (1903–?) was known primarily as a violinist rather than as a conductor. She was trained at the Royal College of Music, where she eventually taught. Wilson was a member of the BBC Orchestra from 1930 to 1944 and occasionally served as its conductor. She founded the Marie Wilson String Quartet (Judy Hill, second violin; Hope Hambourg, viola; Lily Phillips, cello) (Palmer, 264).

The **New York Ladies Ensemble** should not be confused with the Women's Chamber Orchestra of New York founded in 1937 by Jeanette Scheerer (See *Women in Music,* November 1936, September 1936).

Ammer (p. 204) gives some interesting information and background on this two-sentence entry concerning the **Musicians' Union** and the **Atlantic Garden Orchestra.**
Originally chartered in 1864, the Mutual Musical Protective Union became affiliated in July 1903 with the American Federation of Labor, which required that it admit women, and from that time on it always included some women members. The first women to join what is today called the American Federation of Musicians were harpists from the New York Metropolitan Opera; by mid-1940, thirty-one women had joined the union, which had a total of about forty-five hundred members. Each member had to pay a hundred-dollar initiation fee and take an examination of musical ability; only two or three applicants failed to pass. Ten of the new women members belonged to the Ladies Elite Orchestra of the Atlantic Garden.

| NEWS, FACTS, ACTIVITIES | WOMEN IN MUSIC | NO CRUSADING NO PLEADING |

Vol. 1. — No. 7   *Edited by Frederique Joanne Petrides*   MARCH, 1936

WHAT WILL HAPPEN AFTER ANOTHER WAR?

Sir Henry Wood, the prominent English conductor, saw no earthly reason why he should dismiss the women players whom he had admitted in the ranks of his Queen's Hall Symphony during the World War.

What if those artists were not men? He had found them to be hard-working, capable and reliable musicians. Their presence in the orchestra had improved the tonal qualities of its strings. Furthermore, the men played the better for competition.

True, the War was over and his women players had been hired in emergency days. But now with peace restored, and the Tommies back from the battlefields, the London musical marts were full of idle men musicians. And, since something had to be done to reduce unemployment, the majority in the profession felt and insisted that Sir Wood should fill all his choirs with men musicians.

But, Sir Wood was not in the least willing to yield. He had always held that sex discrimination has no place in music and the arts. What if the majority of his fellow-conductors and musicians in England, did not agree with him on this subject? He was not going to sacrifice his principles for the sake of precedent. Accordingly, he stood determinedly by his female instrumentalists—a stand which infuriated the opposition. So much so, indeed, that by 1924, all English musical unions were closed to women.

Faced with such developments, women musicians in London retaliated by forming not only a musical union of their own, but the British Women's Symphony Orchestra as well under Miss Gwynne Kimpton. The Orchestra, a co-operative enterprise, was under the immediate patronage of the Queen. It made its debut in the spring of 1924 and has been commendably active ever since.

"A STATELY BLONDE woman violinist, Marie Wilson, has been chosen director of the Promenade Concert Orchestra, organized by the British Broadcasting Company and composed of ninety musicians, only eleven of whom are women.

"In reporting the choice of Miss Wilson as director, the *Transradio Press Service* says that she has 'none of the tiresome little mannerisms which make many violinists a trial to watch.'"—*Equal Rights.*"

For The Record !

Five hundred and twenty-two women musicians are affiliated with the eight women's orchestras which function now in America. Listed in the chronological order of their inception, these groups are:

Los Angeles Women's Symphony: 70 players. — Philadelphia Women's Orchestra: 60 players. — Women's Symphony of Long Beach, Cal.: 105 players. — Woman's Symphony of Chicago: 100 players.—Orchestrette Classique: 24 players. — Portland Women: 35 players. — N. Y. Women's Orchestra: 85 players. — Women's Little Symphony of Cleveland: 43 players.

The above list does not include women's jazz orchestras or chamber groups of less than fifteen players.

Here and There

"One more girl-band is about all this country needs to send it right back into the depths of the depression" and other similar samples of soporific witticisms on women musicians and women's jazz orchestras, run through a childish short story which appeared some few weeks ago in the *Saturday Evening Post* under the caption "Special Arrangement."

* * *

Newcomer in the field: The N. Y. Ladies' Ensemble. 12 players with Giulietta Morino as the leading violinist.

* * *

Commenting on the recently celebrated tenth anniversary of the Woman's Symphony of Chicago, *Time*, the news-magazine, said that Miss Sundstrom's group was started by three players in it, who collected $1.000 from Samuel Insull, an equal amount from the late Julius Rosenwald and persuaded Richard Czernonky of Bush Conservatory to be their first conductor.

* * *

The N. Y. Women's Symphony is scheduled to close its second season with a concert on April 14.

* * *

The first group of New York women players to join the Musicians' Union back in 1903, was the Atlantic Garden Orchestra. The Orchestra played only popular music.

* * *

The story of the "Orchestrette Classique" will be told in the next issue of *Women in Music.*

CLEVELAND WOMEN LAUNCH SYMPHONY

CLEVELAND, O.—The Women's Little Symphony of Cleveland, conducted by Miss Ruth Sandra Rothstein, is the latest addition to the musical life of this city. Organized last November, the Orchestra is composed of 43 young players. It made its initial bow on January 8th, at the Little Theatre of the Public Hall before an enthusiastic audience.

At the beginning, the task of finding all the needed players presented serious difficulties. Cleveland has never been without its quota of well trained and experienced women players. It so happened, however, that when approached, most of these did not care to join the orchestra, basing their refusal on loyalty to various musical groups to which they had belonged for years. Fortunately, Miss Rothstein was able to cope with this situation by recruiting about twenty of her players among students.

"Naturally, now that we have started, many of our local women musicians, who, up to a few months ago were not interested in the orchestra, would like to join," said Miss Rothstein to *Women in Music*. "But, I am not willing to let down the capable and hard-working youngsters who started out with me in the face of great competition".

The Little Symphony enjoys the support of a women's committee. It is well disciplined and is determined to make its performances truly noteworthy from the artistic standpoint. Its spirit is of the finest and it has in Miss Rothstein a conductor who combines leadership with taste and fine musicianship.

Miss Rothstein received her musical training in Boston, Lausanne and Berlin. Before coming to Cleveland, she led the Boston Women's Little Symphony for the season of 1933. She believes that the day will come when Cleveland will be justifiably proud of her orchestra.

NEW YORK CITY. — About four thousand persons, gathered in the Ballroom of the Waldorf Astoria for the annual Charity affair of the Metropolitan Florists' Association on March 4, listened to a brief concert given by the Orchestrette Classique, under the conductorship of Frederique Joanne Petrides.

With this and similar engagements on its record, the Orchestrette has been heard by some nine thousand persons since last October, besides, of course, its Aeolian Hall audiences.

Published by the "Orchestrette Classique", 190 East End Ave., New York City.

A program from the 1936 **Women's Little Symphony of Cleveland** states:

> The Women's Little Symphony was organized for the purpose of developing and presenting the best talent among Cleveland's young women instrumentalists. With the inception of this organization, Cleveland's first Women's Symphony Orchestra, an opportunity is provided for women to perform major orchestral works within their scope.

Second Season   1927-28   Third Concert

The
Womans
Symphony
Orchestra
of Chicago

ETHEL LEGINSKA
Conductor

Goodman Theatre, February 5, 1928

8:15 p. m.

Management BERTHA OTT, *Inc.*

Curiously, there is no correspondence extant concerning this "novel gesture." It was a busy time for the **Long Beach** group and Whitaker, Anderson's husband-manager, wrote to Petrides giving many details of their concerts and schedule for May 1936. For a May 4 concert, they expected an audience of five thousand. On May 20 the Southern California Symposium of Music (members were orchestra conductors from "the southland") planned to use the Women's Symphony "to see what makes it tick." One would assume this was a workshop for conductors. Anderson and Whitaker did visit New York in August, which Petrides noted in *Women in Music* (August 1936).

In 1936 Petrides wrote **Gertrude Herliczka** concerning her role as a correspondent.

> In years to come, when *Women in Music* will be established and well known over two continents, I promise to spare my friends of the necessity of helping me gather the news. . . . Did you ever imagine yourself in the part of a European correspondent for a music magazine? Yet, this is what you actually are: the continental editor of *Women in Music*.

Austrian-born Herliczka and Petrides corresponded frequently. The only letters that remain span April 1935 through September 1937. Herliczka's letters are full of details of her personal life as well as her career. Her husband's name was Hoffman, and she wrote of one son, Peter. She and Petrides had much in common, for both were professional conductors and married—though only their gender made this combination unusual. They frequently discussed conductorial problems and programming as well as the attitudes of their husbands toward their careers.

On the subject of conflict between personal and professional lives, Herliczka wrote in 1935 that Petrides could tell her husband Peter that he was not the only one who had a talented wife and that after all it was only right that men adjust themselves to women as women to men. She later asked Petrides if her husband was supportive and suggested that hers was, although "he renounced too many activities." However, she observed, he benefited by her professional life because she could never stand a quiet "houselife and leave off" her musical or intellectual interests.

Herliczka once advised Petrides to hire well-known soloists rather than use personnel from within the organization. In a discussion concerning emotional preparation before a concert, she confided that she hated arriving

| NEWS, FACTS, ACTIVITIES | # WOMEN IN MUSIC | NO CRUSADING NO PLEADING |

Vol. 1.—No. 8   *Edited by Frederique Joanne Petrides*   MAY, 1936

WHEN ONE NOVELTY OUTSHONE ANOTHER!

There was a time when "painless tooth extraction" proved a serious competitor, in terms of audience, to a women's orchestra. Consider, for instance, the following incident. It occurred during the early days of the Los Angeles Women's Symphony.

In 1896, after its formal debut, the Orchestra went to give an afternoon concert in Santa Ana. There is no doubt that the news of the impending event must have intrigued the imagination of many persons in that peaceful California community. Feminine orchestras were the novelty in those days and times, which tradition would have one associate with glamor, gaiety and what not.

One may then well visualize music lovers and crowds of curiosity seekers in Santa Ana rushing on the day of the performance to "see and hear" the visiting and truly pioneering women musicians from Los Angeles.

"The hall was brilliantly decorated for this occasion and the feminine artists were in charming attire," says Caroline Estes Smith, in her book on the 'Los Angeles Philarmonic Orchestra'. All was in readiness, but there were more people in the orchestra than in the audience.

"Competition could be heard in the street below, where at frequent intervals during the afternoon some one played vigorously on a guitar and 'fiddle'. The audience which had been expected upstairs surrounded a crude wagon in the street where it was discovered that a painless 'tooth puller' was conducting a hastily improvised dental office with his chair and other paraphernalia in the wagon, and every time a patient had a tooth extracted there were vociferous shouts and loud applause by the spectators while the itinerant musicians whanged away in happy celebration."

THANKS to a novel gesture from the other end of the land, four Juilliard students in New York will attend, as the guests of the Long Beach, California, Woman's Orchestra, the May 11 concert of the Orchestrette. "We too were an unendowed group dependent upon our own resources, but faith and determination has made us the largest in the land," Eva Anderson, leader of the ten-year-old California venture of 105 players, stated to the Orchestrette in remitting for the tickets.

Believe It Or Not!

Men pianists are not effeminate, of course, but there is an Oxford tradition that at an amateur concert about the year 1827, the performance of the first male pianist that had been seen or heard in the celebrated English University was greeted with hisses, according to Eva Mary Grew, associate editor of *The British Musician*. The pianoforte was then regarded as essentially a woman's instrument; hence the hissing.

Here and There

Are male musicians in America to be blamed entirely for the non-inclusion of more than a few women in symphony orchestras? No. . . they are not, as *Women in Music* will attempt to prove in one of its forthcoming issues.

* * *

Besides its economic benefits, the inclusion of women musicians in WPA orchestras, also has an important educational angle. It enables, for instance, various conductors and players to find out for themselves whether women can or cannot be depended upon to do their share well as orchestral artists.

* * *

As a result of temporary lapse in all needed support, the N. Y. Woman's Symphony went through some difficult and trying weeks in the course of its second season, which ended with a concert in Carnegie Hall on April 14. Thanks, however, to the idealism of its players and the determination of Miss Antonia Brico, their conductor, the orchestra remained intact—a feat which deserves congratulations.

* * *

Mildred Seydell, noted Southern writer, whose daily comments in the *Atlanta Georgian* are widely read, extended, on March 31, her department's hospitality to Frederique Joanne Petrides on the subject of conductors, orchestras and players on the distaff side.

* * *

The "fraternal kiss"; also, the approving and complimentary words. which "Big Brother" *Musical Courier* extended editorially in its issue of April 4 to *Women in Music*, are hereby thankfully acknowledged.

ORCHESTRETTE ENDS THIRD SEASON

NEW YORK CITY. — The axiom that many things can be attained once a group resolves to work for an ideal, a goal, also applies in the case of the Orchestrette Classique, — a woman's miniature symphony which ends its third season with a concert on Monday evening, May 11, at Aeolian Hall.

The Orchestrette was founded in 1933 by Miss Frederique Joanne Petrides, its conductor. Started with a nucleus of six, it is now composed of 24 young musicians. Although self-managed and functioning with no subsidy or endowment, it has succeeded, nevertheless, in covering most of its expenses and also in yielding definite earnings to its players.

The ensemble plays music written by the masters of all periods. Last winter, however, it broadened its scope by including works of contemporary Americans in its concerts. One of these composers is Julia Smith, the group's pianist.

Since October, 1935, the venture has widened considerably the circle of those who are familiar with its work. Thus, besides its regular concerts, it also played for various educational and social groups, with the result that it reached some additional nine thousand persons.

The concert with which the Orchestrette will close its third season on May 11 features two soloists — both drawn from its own ranks. These are: Hinde Barnett, the ensemble's concert master, and Ruth Cubbage, flautist. Other participating artists are: Anne Berger Littman, Rebecca Merritt, Florence Nicolaides, Shirley Portnoi, Lillian Rosenfield, Zena Scherer, Susan Kessler, Virginia Payton, Carolyn Potter, Josephine La Prade, Erika Kutzing, Helen Enser, Anne Brown, Julia Smith, Lois Wann, Margaret Schillinger Rosov and Ilene Skolnak.

PARIS.—A good cause for reflection was given to concert-going Frenchmen by Gertrud Hrdliczka, the Viennese-American conductor, throughout this season. Her concerts on the air, at the Opera Comique and at the Russian Festival enthused and surprised her listeners, who, unlike Americans, have not been very friendly in the past to the work of women conductors. President Le Brun was one of the many celebrities who complimented Miss Hrdliczka on her work.

Published by the "Orchestrette Classique", 190 East End Ave., New York City.

at the hall early and found ten minutes before curtain to be about right. In 1937 she wrote of having made big professional strides, for she was conducting with the best-known conductors of the times—Bruno Walter, Kleicher, Furtwängler, Mollnari, De Sabata, etc.

Petrides with the Orchestrette Classique.

Stokowski could easily have been influenced by his wife, Olga Samaroff.

Alice Wagener, director of the **Girl Scout** camp wrote that while they appreciated the wonderful concert they could not offer any remuneration. Wagener did plan to ask the National Headquarters to send fifteen dollars for transportation expenses.

In March 1936 Whitaker, husband of **Long Beach Woman's Symphony** conductor **Eva Anderson**, wrote that

> . . . for such a huge group, and it being composed of young, immature musicians our orchestra performed like veterans and professionals. The audience was a *Who's Who* of the west. . . . The conductor [Harley Hamilton] of the Los Angeles Women's Symphony was present . . . and not usually given to compliments of any kind and on the contrary being noted for destructive criticisms, he had nothing but praise.

Whitaker continued by recounting the problems of flu and mumps epidemics. "My concern," he stated, "principally is to keep the conductor on her feet—she gets 'low' at times too, but I really believe she'd rise in her shroud to see a concert thru if it were billed for the next day after she quits breathing."

In another letter dated April 2, 1936, he spoke of a proposed Honolulu trip and the possibility of attending the Texas Centennial in Dallas. He reported widespread fatigue within their group and the necessity of a "tongue-lashing just before the curtain." Whitaker named their small groups as follows: the Cecilians, the Carolinans, the Criterions, the Novelettes, and "Eve's Own Imperial Quartet."

According to Ammer (p.114), Simonis founded the **Pittsburgh Woman's Symphony** in 1934.

Lady Folkestone (Helen Radnor, Viscountess of Folkestone) was a late nineteenth- to twentieth-century English conductor, editor, singer, and composer. She aided in founding the Royal College of Music, London, and organized "a ladies string band and chorus, giving numerous charity concerts" (Cohen, 570).

Grace Burrows conducted the **British Women's Symphony Orchestra** from 1933 through 1935.

| NEWS, FACTS, ACTIVITIES | # WOMEN IN MUSIC | NO CRUSADING NO PLEADING |

Vol. II. No. 1   *Edited by Frederique Petrides*   JULY, 1936

HUMOROUS OR NOT, HERE THEY ARE!

This column believes that *Women in Music* should print from time to time anecdotes on women conductors and women orchestras. Accordingly, it feels no hesitation in presenting the following two items, the first of which pertains to the players of an out-of-town orchestra.

After this particular orchestra had been organized, a dressmaker was asked to make uniform gowns for its players. She made such an elegant and flattering job that the ladies started wearing her creation for social functions as well. In consequence, the costumes were practically all worn out by the beginning of the following season, a calamity which caused a repeat order to the dressmaker. But, it so happened, that at the end of the year the musicians had to have new professional attire again. Just then a wealthy woman offered to pay for new gowns, provided she could design them. Although about five years have passed since the thoughtful lady designed and donated the dresses, the girls are still using them, but only while giving concerts. They look so forbidding and nun-like in them that they have never dared use them socially. In fact, they despise the sight of these dresses and the sooner they will get new and smart looking ones, the better it will be for their feminine self-respect and their perturbed peace of mind.

The second story is about Antonia Brico, the conductor, who while rehearsing, not so long ago, a New York WPA all-man orchestra, heard certain players talk among themselves. When she asked them to keep quiet, her command was greeted with innocent laughter. Why that mirth? Miss Brico forgot that the orchestra was not her N. Y. Woman's Symphony and she had thrust at the jabbering males the words: "A little more quiet, *girls!*"

STOKOWSKI is not the only first-rank conductor in America who has publicly lauded the merits of women as musicians and more specifically as orchestral players. Serge Koussevitzky, the world-renowned conductor of the Boston Symphony, also spoke a few years ago on the "greater appreciativeness and responsiveness of women as regards the conductor's intentions" and stressed especially the point that "their presence in an orchestra conduces to good discipline in the ranks."

--And We Still Pay!

Orchestras in music minded ancient Egypt often numbered 600 instruments and included about 12,000 persons in their supporting choruses. Not only women did also play in these orchestras, but they gradually superseded the male artists in them.

Here and There

"Would it not be a fine thing if women orchestras in this country would form a close association or organisation of their own? The interchange of ideas etc., etc., would decidedly be a forward movement to give women their proper place in music," writes Mr. Carl Simonis, the third conductor in the field, thus far, to make such a suggestion to *Women in Music.*

* * *

Audiences of 40,000 persons are expected to attend the outdoor concerts which the Woman's Symphony of Chicago will give again this summer at Grant Park. The group is led by Ebba Sundstrom, who recently guest conducted the Philadelphia Civic Orchestra.

* * *

The July issue of *The American Music Lover* contains an article on "Women Conductors". The piece is a contribution of Frederique Petrides, conductor of the Orchestrette Classique.

* * *

Girl Scout executives and leaders assembled at their Camp Edith Macy National Training School in Briarcliff Manor, N. Y., heard on Sunday, June 7, a concert by the Orchestrette Classique. Incidentally, the strings of this orchestra are at present recording old music for the Columbia Phonograph Recording Company.

* * *

The busiest ensemble of its kind is the Long Beach, Cal,. Woman's Symphony. Closing its spring season on June 14 with two concerts at St. Bernardino, this orhchestra will play again at the San Diego Exposition on August 23. Eva Anderson is the conductor.

* * *

Two Washington. D. C., letters to *Women in Music,* the one from Dr. Nikolai Sokoloff, Federal Director of WPA Music Projects, the other from Mrs. Roberta Campbell Lawson, President of the General Federation of Women's Clubs, comment favorably on the contents of this publication, which, beginning with the present issue, enters its second year.

FIVE HARP PLAYERS IN NEW ORCHESTRA

PITTSBURGH, PA.—The third orchestra of women to be launched in Pennsylvania in the last 16 years has its headquarters in this city and functions under Mr. Carl Simonis. Starting last October with 12 players, the Pittsburgh Woman's Symphony is now composed of 50 instrumentalists and looks forward to a busy schedule next season.

This novel addition to our local musical activities plays only popular classic music and has to its credit a number of well attended concerts, which have evoked an enthusiastic response.

Discussing the scope of the group, Mr. Simonis said to *Women in Music:* —"We are not here to compete in any way or shape with our admirable Pittsburgh Symphony. This we have made very plain, indeed, as we are anxious to avoid any unnecessary criticism. Naturally, it is no secret that for this or that reason, most of our major Symphonies employ women only as harpists. Our orchestra, therefore, aims to give its players proper opportunities to avail themselves of their talents and acqured knowledge. It fills a need and, consequently, deserves all encouragement."

The Orchestra employs 5 harpists, most of whom are temporarily filling the gaps caused by the presence of only two players in the bass section. It is believed, however, that it will be possible to find more doublebass participants in the near future.

(Ed. Note: The two post-war orchestras which have preceded the Pittsburgh group in Pennsylvania are: the Philadelphia Woman's Symphony, founded in 1921, and the Erie Woman's Little Symphony, organized in 1920 by C. D. Gianfoni, who in 1935 was given charge of the Los Angeles Woman's Orchestra from which he has resigned a few weeks ago, according to latest reports from the Western Coast.)

LONDON. — Recent professional activities of no less than four English women conductors have made many an old-timer reminisce about the harsh treatment meted out to valiant Lady Folkestone at the time she dared conduct a Symphony here some fifty years ago. However, times and viewpoints do change and the reception accorded to the four women orchestral leaders was very cordial. One of these artistes is Grace Burrows, the new maestra of the British Women's Symphony.

Published by the "Orchestrette Classique", 190 East End Ave., New York City.

The famous Italian **Bembo** family is not thought to be related to Antonia Bembo, an Italian composer. When Petrides discussed Antonia (*Women in Music,* April 1940), she misspelled her name "Bambo."

To have the support of **Leopold Stokowski** must have given the **Philadelphia Women's Symphony** a confidence not enjoyed by many of the other women's orchestras. A major concern of many of these ensembles centered around presenting a nonthreatening posture to the established municipal orchestras. In 1912 Stokowski was appointed conductor of the Philadelphia Orchestra, which was enjoying the reputation of being one of the world's best orchestras. He frequently spoke about the merits of women as musicians and orchestral players (*Women in Music,* July 1936) but Ammer (p. 202) points out that, while he declared in 1916

> that not hiring women constituted a terrible waste of 'splendid power,' . . . he himself did not engage one until 1930—and the first non harpist (cellist Elsa Hilger) only in 1936—although his reign over the Philadelphia Orchestra had been undisputed since 1912. (He later vindicated himself, for the American Symphony Orchestra, which he founded in 1962, from the beginning included many women and also many blacks and members of other minority groups.)

> Hilger's brochure states she was hired in 1935.

| NEWS, FACTS, ACTIVITIES | # WOMEN IN MUSIC | NO CRUSADING NO PLEADING |

Vol. II. No. 2.   *Edited by Frederique Petrides*   AUGUST, 1936

THE GOOD OLD DAYS WERE NOT SO GOOD!

In these days when a musical education for the young lady in the family is taken to be a major cultural necessity in the judgement of progressive parents, the following letter, written around 1500 by Pietro Bembo, an Italian poet, to his daughter Elena, offers an interesting contrast:

".... Concerning your fervent wish to allow you to play the monochord, I have to tell you a few things of which, owing to your tender age, you are no doubt ignorant," wrote the poet to his offspring. "To play music," he continued, "is the thing that a vain, superficial and loose woman does and I want you to be known as the woman with the most honor and the biggest modesty that has ever lived. Besides, if you play badly, music will give you little joy and bring you only disgrace. But to play well, that you can accomplish only if you devote 10 or 12 years to your studies without doing anything else besides. To my way of thinking, it is enough that you feel at home in literature and in the kitchen."

So much for music for many Elenas of yesteryears.

But what about gentlemen of other days whose wives were public singers?

In his scintillating "Life of Johnson," Boswell speaks of a young gentleman in the 18th century, "who had not a shilling in the world" but who was determined that his bride—'an eminent singer'—should no longer sing in public. Johnson heard of this and "with all the high spirit of a Roman Senator, exclaimed, 'He resolved wisely and nobly to be sure. He is a brave man. Would not a gentleman be disgraced by having his wife singing publickly for hire? No, Sir, there can be no doubt here. I know not if I should not prepare myself for a publick singer as readily as let my wife be one'."

COMMENTING on the non-inclusion of women cellists in the personnel of the celebrated British Broadcasting Company's Orchestra, Dame Smyth, the sharp-tongued English composer and writer, made in 1933 the following provocative remark. "The B.B.C. has plenty of women in its fine band. But here is a strange thing: in that orchestra, women cellists are banned. Why, I cannot conceive .... perhaps the *attitude* of the cello player is considered an unseemly one for women?"

On the Job!

During their recent stay in New York, Eva Anderson, conductor of the Long Beach, California, Woman's Symphony and Herbert Whitaker, her husband-manager, had this story to tell: "The Sunday after the Long Beach earthquake, when everybody was shaken out of house and home, our orchestra managed to assemble and play an outdoor concert for the quake refugees. This, despite the fact that many of the girl-players were themselves homeless, too."

Here and There

Evidently, not every French aristocrat has drained the cup of knowledge. For instance: At a symphony concert held some few months ago at the most exclusive Club in Paris and conducted by Gertrude Herliczka, an elderly lady in the audience was overheard asking her escort: "What is that young lady with the stick in her hand doing in front of the orchestra?" — "She is conducting, Madame!"—"But, what is the sense of having a conductor since all these musicians already know how to play by themselves?" the old lady wondered.

. . .

It seems that there still remain a few things that find favor with the politicians of both major parties. Thus, women's bands were heard and cheered by Democrats and Republicans alike at their respective National Conventions.

. . .

Two of New York City's feminine orchestras — the Woman's Symphony conducted by Antonia Brico, and the Orchestrette Classique, conducted by Frederique Petrides, will each give three concerts next season.

. . .

About 25,000 club women heard on July 17 a concert in Chicago's Grant Park Shell given by their local Woman's Symphony and broadcast over WJZ. Claire Page, "one of Chicago's best publicity writers," is the orchestra's business manager.

. . .

The Gabrielle Horn Quartet should prove a welcome novelty in the New York ensemble field. Helen Enser, first horn player of the Orchestrette, Frieda Eissman, Ellen Stone and Suzanne Howitt are its players.

. . .

From conductor Quinto Maganini: —"I enjoyed reading *Women in Music* and I always appreciate anything that gives me some new knowledge."

STOKOWSKI'S ZEAL LED TO ORCHESTRA

Philadelphia, Pa. — A survey of available local feminine talent, undertaken in 1920 by Mrs. Mabel Swint Ewer of this city at Mr. Stokowski's personal recommendation, resulted in the course of a few months in the formation of the Philadelphia Woman's Symphony Orchestra. This organization made its debut in January, 1921, under the direction of Mr. J. W. F. Leman, who still is its regular conductor.

Many women, prominent in local social and musical circles, are playing in the orchestra, which limits its ranks to 70 pieces and aims to offer exceptional opportunities to its players for the study of the best orchestral music. Nationally known musicians have often conducted it as guests and many outstanding artists have been among its soloists. All players in the group are unsalaried, but the goal now is toward an adequate compensation.

Mr. Leman, who also leads the Frankford Symphony Orchestra and the Little Symphony of Philadelphia, said to *Women in Music:* "So successfully has our orchestra been received that an endowment was proposed a month before the financial crash in 1929, which subsequently was abandoned until the return of normal conditions. However, the orchestra has weathered the financial depression and plans have been formulated to make an effort next season to place it on a firmer financial backing."

Founder Mrs. Ewer played the trumpet in the orchestra for 8 years. She is still interested in the group, being the chairman of the auxiliary Board of Directors. Other officer-players are: Miss E. Laura Hannum, President and one of the first violins; Miss Eleanor Riedegir, vice-President (flute); Miss Elizabeth Harris, Secretary, (oboe); Miss Katherine Sullivan, Treasurer, (violin).

SOONER or later there will be an undersupply of adequately trained male musicians in the symphonic field. Due to technological unemployment, music is no desirable career for the man who must earn a living. Consequently, few will or can choose it as a profession and here lies the opportunity denied women since history began, according to an *Independent Woman* article by Mr. R. Pantzer, a conductor, now doing musical research for the State Museum at Jefferson City, Mo.

Published by the "Orchestrette Classique", 190 East End Ave., New York City.

VOL. II, NO. 3, NOVEMBER 1936

Dutch composer, conductor, and lecturer **Elizabeth Kuyper** (1877–1953) was a pupil of Barth and Max Bruch at the Berlin Hochschule where she taught theory and composition from 1908 to 1920. In 1908 she founded and conducted a women's orchestra in Berlin and also conducted the New York Women's Symphony and the London Women's Symphony Orchestra. Kuyper worked and lived in New York for a number of years and later returned to Europe.

The ***Billboard*** was advertised as being the "World's Foremost Amusement Weekly." Paul Denis, the associate editor, had attended the debut of the Orchestrette at Aeolian May 14, 1934, and commented that he had been "pleasantly surprised," finding the concert an exciting experience, and due to Petrides's "painstaking" conducting he thought it a memorable concert. He then made his suggestion concerning women in jazz. His guide for proper conduct for "girl dance band musicians" can be found quoted in *Women in Music,* April 15, 1939.

Jeannette Scheerer's orchestra was called the New York Chamber Orchestra (*Women in Music,* September 1937).

Canadian born **Gena Branscombe** (1881–1977) lived most of her life in the United States. She studied composition and piano at the Chicago Musical College. In 1907 she moved to Washington state and served as head of the piano department at Whitman College for two years. She later became interested in conducting and studied with Frank Damrosch and Albert Stoessel. She married John Ferguson Tenney from New York in 1910, and they had four daughters. In 1933 she formed the Branscombe Chorale, for which she wrote and arranged many works. She conducted this group, giving annual Town Hall concerts until 1954. Branscombe published many works but is perhaps best known for her choral work *Coventry's Choir,* written for women's chorus and orchestra. She was always a vigorous supporter of women musicians and once said, "Having a home, a husband, and children to love and serve brings enrichment of life to a woman, but being a part of the world's work in humbly serving and loving the illumined force which is music brings fulfillment."

Later, in 1962, she wrote,

> Had there been time, space, money, I could have done hundreds of programs devoted entirely to the works, large and small, of women composers. I have found women, in groups and individually, generous,

WOMEN IN MUSIC

NO CRUSADING
NO PLEADING

Vol. II. No. 3. *Edited by Frederique Petrides* NOVEMBER, 1936

LACK OF SUPPORT DOOMED HER WORK

Elizabeth Kuyper, a courageous musician who founded and led in 1910 a Woman's Orchestra in Berlin, must have been keenly disappointed when she found out that every violinist in her group wanted to be the concert-master or sit, at least, at the first desks. And, as if such an anomalous situation was not sufficiently unpleasant, she also discovered that most girls hated to play the viola because they had small hands; that older players were sensitive to matters of priority and respect and that the atmosphere surrounding her work was full of jealousies.

However, being endowed with tact and diplomacy, Madame Kuyper managed, in due course of time, to iron out all her internal organizational problems and the orchestra, the second to be started in Berlin since the end of the "nineties", started giving public performances which soon attracted cordial comments for their excellent work.

The ensemble included 65 players. Most of its wind and all of its brass instruments were played by men, who offered the utmost co-operation, never missed a rehearsal and were the first to admit that the string sections were ideal from the standpoint of tonal quality, feeling and response to their conductor's demands. Nevertheless, despite her group's artistic merits, Madame Kuyper was unable to secure the necessary financial backing for it. She kept paying all the expenses out of her own earnings as music teacher. At the end, she abandoned the venture and a few years after the World War tried to launch a woman's Symphony in New York.

Here, too, her venture was doomed to fail. No hordes of wealthy music-lovers responded to her appeals for its support. Consequently, the orchestra disbanded soon after its units were completed.

"I HAVE been getting your charming little *Women in Music* and I am pleasantly surprised to know that women are so active and doing such fine work in the concert field...But, if suggestions from men are proper in a woman's publication, I think it would be a good thing to devote more space to women in jazz music. There are such outstanding women musicians in this particular field as Ina Ray Hutton, Rita Rio and Betty Beal (all leaders of headline jazz bands) ...," writes Mr. Paul Denis, Associate Editor of *The Billboard*.

For The Record!

Sixteen women orchestral conductors led concerts in various parts of the world during the last twelve months. Four of the these musicians live in London, England; two in New York; two in Chicago; two in Paris; two in Vienna; one in Moscow; one in Cleveland, Ohio; one in Long Beach, Cal., and one in Portland, Oregon.

Here and There

A reader reports that the August issue of *Women in Music* was read by Prof. Vincent Jones to the students of one of his summer classes at the New York University. There followed a discussion as to whether women should or should not lead, or play, in orchestras. The verdict was that *woman's place is in the kitchen!!!*

* * *

The first of the three Orchestrette Classique concerts for the season 1936-1937 will be given on Monday, Nov. 30th, at the Carnegie Chamber Music Hall in New York. The program will include Gretry's Concerto for the flute. Frederique Petrides will conduct the group, which inaugurates its fourth season. Lorna Wren, flutist, will be the assisting artist.

* * *

The New York Woman's Symphony opens its third season at Carnegie Hall on December 1st....Jeannette Scheerer, the noted clarinetist, has started a woman's orchestra which employs 28 players......Ethel Stark, violinist, is rehearsing a new concert group composed of 14 women players.

* * *

Gena Branscombe has recently conducted a program of her own orchestral and choral works, including her symphonic suite "Quebec", over Station CRCY (Toronto).

* * *

Headed by Hinda Barnett, the Orchestrette String Quartet, played, on October 10, at the Westport (Conn.) home of Mr. John Chapman, the well-known N. Y. columnist.

* * *

Musical Nuisances: Leaders of woman's orchestras in the concert field, who don't at least attempt to offer interesting programs because they obviously believe that most music-lovers still like to be sentimental and uncritical regarding the work of feminine orchestral ensembles.

"MUSICAL AMAZONS" ACTIVE IN PARIS

PARIS, France.— Unlike London, Berlin and Vienna where woman's orchestras functioned even before the World War, the first Parisian ladies' orchestra was inaugurated as late as the spring of 1930. Known as the Woman's Orchestra of Paris, this ensemble emerged under the command of Jane Evrard, a young violinist, who, incidentally, is the first French woman to lead, professionally, an orchestra here.

At the beginning, many Parisians regarded the venture as a noble and charming joke. They doubted whether a woman conductor could ever possess "the wisdom and the executive qualities of a Solon" with which to keep together "her graceful phalanx of musical amazons" and felt that sooner or later "woman's rugged individualism" would assert itself at the expense of the orchestra's existence. But those fears and doubts have long since been dispelled. Instead of disbanding, the orchestra is still active and is now quite noted for its programs which combine classical and contemporary music.

Early in 1933, Madame Evrard's group, composed of 23 string players, toured Spain. When the news of its successes in Madrid, Bilbao, Oviedo, Valencia and Tarragona started adorning the pages of the Paris press, Frenchmen experienced feelings of pardonable pride over the achievements of their feminine musical compatriots.

(Ed. Note: Composers Augusta Holmes and Cecile Chaminade were among the first French women who led, although non-professionally, orchestras in Paris. Gertrude Herliczka, the Viennese-American, and Carmen Studer Weingartner, wife of Felix Weingartner, are among Madame Evrard's non-French contemporaries who also have conducted professionally in the French Capitol.)

PORTLAND, Oregon.— Basing his argument on the inadvisability of having a woman's symphony orchestra in a city where even such an established organization as the Portland Symphony cannot be maintained on a strictly professional basis, Dr. Nikolai Sokoloff, speaking at a luncheon sponsored by our local Woman's Symphony, frowned upon "segregation of the sexes" in musical matters and urged that women who are good musicians should become members of the Portland Symphony Orchestra which employs both men and women musicians.

Published by the "Orchestrette Classique", 190 East End Ave., New York City.

> chivalrous, efficient, and intelligent—a joy to work with. . . . It's a good life, being a woman composer, worth all the hard work that goes into it. (Ammer, 160–62)

The information from Europe about **Jane Evrard** (earlier referred to as Jeannette) came from Herliczka, who informed Petrides about Evrard, other European conductors and her own activities. In a later letter (July 10, 1937) she told of attending a concert that Evrard was scheduled to conduct, but when Herliczka arrived she found Evrard's name scratched out in pencil and "a terrible old man conducted."

Herliczka described Evrard as a "society woman" but also stated that her work as a conductor was "absolutely serious," the orchestra was good, and she had "quite a following."

Another reference to Evrard came in correspondence from George Maynard, a composer whose music Petrides had performed. He generally had disparaging words for women composers and musicians (referring to "Nannerl" Mozart as "that Mozart girl") but wrote that in 1933, he had heard Jane Evrard's orchestra do a new Honegger work at the École Normale and that the concert was decidedly impressive.

Ruth Stuber playing timpani, 1940. Courtesy of the Philadelphia Inquirer.

VOL. II, NO. 4, JANUARY 1937

Petrides's research and subsequent article is an excellent example of the kind of information she thought so important for her readers. In fact, the **Vienna Ladies Orchestra** came back to the United States in 1873 and ". . . they were roaming about the land as 'lager-beer musicians,' playing in restaurants and beer gardens." After their tours, many American women imitated the Vienna Ladies and were especially popular in areas where there were large settlements of German-Americans (Ammer, 102).

Phil Spitalny (1890–1970) was a Ukrainian-born, American conductor who formed a women's orchestra in 1934. His wife, **Evelyn**, with her "magic violin" (a Bergonzi), was his featured soloist. From 1935 to 1948 the orchestra had its own radio program called the "Hour of Charm." Although Petrides calls the group a jazz orchestra, the repertory they played was mostly "sweet" arrangements of light classical music. Each program opened and closed with a hymn sung by all the players. The orchestra performed in several short films and in *Here Come the Coeds* (1945) before disbanding in the early 1950s.

Ethel Bartlett and **Rae Robertson** were a husband and wife duo-piano team from England.

According to a 1936–37 promotional leaflet, **Willem Durieux**, a cellist, founded and conducted a series of three chamber music concerts each season. Concerts were given at the MacDowell Club of New York, 166 East 73rd Street, tickets were $1.10, and concerts began "at 8:45 o'clock promptly." The programming was impressive and included women's compositions. Personnel that season were: Christine Phillipson, Eugenie Limberg, and Byrd Elyoton on first violin; Marie van den Broeck, Gertrude Buttrey, and Helen Schaffer on second violin; Virginia Coy and Dorothea Bestor on viola; Virginia Nolte and Esther Pierce on violon-cellos; and double-bass—Marjorie Seymour (Clipping Files, NYPL).

Whitaker wrote Petrides in March 1937 of the **Long Beach** group's busy schedule. The group planned to play ". . . Sunday afternoon on the 28th Anniversary concert of the Long Beach Municipal Band . . . a concert that is expected to draw around six or seven thousand people." He noted improvement in their financial situation and mentioned that "the small groups are getting more dates all the time."
His postscript reads,

| NEWS, FACTS, ACTIVITIES | WOMEN IN MUSIC | NO CRUSADING NO PLEADING |

WOMEN IN MUSIC

NEWS, FACTS, ACTIVITIES

NO CRUSADING NO PLEADING

Vol. II. No. 4. *Edited by Frederique Petrides* JANUARY, 1937

VIENNA'S SURPRISE TO OLD NEW YORK

Throughout the twelve days which followed the evening of September 11, 1871, curious crowds of New Yorkers were rushing nightly and on matinee days to the old Steinway Hall on Fourteenth Street. The Vienna Ladies' Orchestra, the only aggregation of its kind to ever visit America, was the performing attraction, the big novelty.

The curiosity over the Vienna Ladies was well justified. Those artists were professionals at a time when, with the exception of isolated cases, the day of the professional woman musician had not yet dawned in America. Besides, their orchestra, not the very first all-feminine ensemble in the history of music, was, nevertheless, the only one of its type heard in America up to that year. Consequently, it stood out as something unique and almost incredible in that period of musical life in the New World.

The visiting group was composed of "twenty artists, most of whom were on the bright side of twenty years of age, generally graceful and good-looking, with sparkling eyes, flowing hair and nimble fingers." These musicians and Josephine Weimlich, their conductor, dressed with the most exquisite taste of their period. They surrounded themselves with "sundry elegant accessories such as roses, white drums and a number of white bouquets of regulation pattern." Their s p e c i a l t y was choice waltz music, although their programs also featured movements from light operas and symphonies. They were brought over by a Mr. Rullman, the first American to manage a woman's orchestra on these shores. Following their New York debut, they were to play in various American cities.

LABOR BULLETIN! The California item in this issue brings to mind, though in contrast, that night in August 1913 when, after having played for three weeks at the Atlantic City Exposition, the players of the celebrated Boston Fadettes Orchestra, (40 women), ascended the stage at concert time, then turned around and walked out again in protest against the Exposition management's failure to pay them their back salaries. Incidentally, this orchestra was founded in Boston shortly before the advent of the "gay nineties."

In Kemal's Country!

An orchestra of sixty women from the Constantinople Conservatory was heard, years ago, by Mr. Ernest Schelling. Quoting him in the music page of the *New York World-Telegram,* critic R. C. Bagar wrote: "The instruments those women played were violins, violas and ouds. The conductor, a man, did not lead with a stick. He had a tambourine of some kind, and he kept the tempo by beating on that. They all played in unison, by the way. There was no such thing as harmony."

Here and There

"How can a person learn to swim, if he is not permitted to go swiming?" Thus wondered Mr. Pierre Key when he outlined in his October *Musical Digest* the plight confronting the worthy but unknown young artist.

* * *

Mr. Key's views prompt this passing mention of the fact that the Orchestrette Classique (Frederique Petrides, conductor) always features as soloists, worthy, although unknown, young musicians, who most assuredly deserve an opportunity to demonstrate their capabilities. Lorna Wren, flutist, was the assisting artist last November. Helen Enser, horn player and a member of the ensemble since 1933, will be its soloist on February 15th at the Carnegie Chamber Music Hall.

* * *

Two more performances are scheduled this season for the New York Women's Symphony, Antonia Brico, conductor, in Carnegie Hall; at the same auditorium, Phil Spitalny's all-girl jazz orchestra will also give a concert in the near future, according to published reports.

* * *

They are having a very exciting time! 'They', being the Woman's Symphony of Chicago, which has engaged artists like Gertrude Wettergren, Ethel Bartlett, Rae Robertson and Carola Goya, the dancer, as soloists for this season. Ebba Sundstrom is the conductor.

* * *

Eleven women players constitute the six year-old Durieux Chamber Ensemble, which will again offer, under the direction of conductor Willem Durieux, programs of unfamiliar music at the MacDowell Club, New York, on Febr. 28th and April 18th.

* * *

"Women in Music", says the *Musical West,* (San Francisco), "is a brochure of decided interest" etc. etc.

STEINER'S HOME TOWN HEARS NEW ENSEMBLE

BALTIMORE, Md.—Musical Baltimore, the birthplace of the late Emma Steiner, who was the first operatic conductor in the history of her sex, heard, on the evening of December 14th, the debut concert of the Women's String Orchestra, a recently organized local ensemble of thirty players. The performance was held at the large-columned gallery of the Art Museum under the leadership of Mr. Stephen Deak, cellist and instructor at the Peabody Conservatory of Music.

Celia Brace, teacher at Peabody's Preparatory Department , is the concertmaster of the orchestra which came to its first performance under handicaps caused by the shortage of available women players for certain instruments. "Chief among these was a scarcity of double-bass players, making it necessary to press into service two players from Philadelphia, who joined the ensemble just in time for two final rehearsals. For pretty much the same reason, apparently, Mr. Deak had the services of only four cellists," remarked the *Baltimore Sun* in its lengthly review of the orchestra's debut.

The program, offering a very interesting selection of little known works for string orchestra, was rendered in a highly satisfactory manner, and was received with genuine appreciation by the large audience which heard it. IDA CAPLES

(Ed. Note: Woman's Symphonic groups in America have now increased to ten, using the services of about 640 players. The largest of these ensembles is in Long Beach, Cal. The Orchestrette Classique, New York, is the smallest. The other groups are in New York, Chicago, Philadelphia, Portland (Oregon), Cleveland, Los Angeles, Pittsburgh and Baltimore.)

LONG BEACH, Cal. — A Gold Medal has been awarded by the California Pacific Exposition to the local Woman's Symphony, Eva Anderson, conductor. In doing so, the Exposition officials stated, through the press, that their choice was unanimous and that they considered no other orchestra for the award. There are 105 players, mainly students, in this organization which was founded in 1925, is sponsored by the City of Long Beach and is one of the busiest training groups on the Pacific Coast.

Published by the "Orchestrette Classique", 190 East End Ave., New York City.

. . . A sad blow to us is the decision of our solo trumpet, Ethel Bennett, to retire. She's only 34 and right at the top in her career, but her husband doesn't like music—and so passes from the picture the best woman trumpeter in the country. Darn some of these husbands. We've lost several good players that way.

Whitaker wrote again in April 1937 that they would regularly be using 120 players. "So many new young musicians are pouring in to us from all over the country that we can pretty well take our pick and choice. . . . The Exposition appearance had a lot to do with the stabilizing of our outfit."

Composer-conductor Emma Steiner. Courtesy Music Division, The
New York Public Library.

Georges Enesco (1881–1955) was a Rumanian composer and violinist. The League of Composers was founded in 1923 in New York. Its main goal was to promote performances of contemporary music.

In this same year conductor Otto Klemperer engaged twenty-year-old **Ellen Stone** as first horn for the Pittsburgh Symphony—an appointment that shattered tradition (*Women in Music,* October 15, 1937). Stone (1917–?) was a student at Juilliard from 1933 to 1936 and studied with Josef Franzl.

American violinist and composer **Carmelita Ippolito** (b. 1902) first appeared in public at the age of five. She studied with C. M. Loeffler at the Juilliard School of Music and E. Zimbalist at the Curtis Institute. Ippolito frequently played on radio broadcasts and toured the United States.

In 1938 **Frederick Huber**, Baltimore's Municipal Orchestra director, wrote to Petrides about the outcome of this conflict. See *Women in Music,* June 1, 1938, for another commentary on this situation.

| NEWS, FACTS, ACTIVITIES | # WOMEN IN MUSIC | NO CRUSADING; NO PLEADING |

Vol. II. No. 5   *Edited by Frederique Petrides*   FEBRUARY, 1937

PIONEER'S RECORD SET FINE EXAMPLE

Emma Steiner, a musician, who passed away five years ago this month in New York, will undoubtedly be hailed by music historians in the future as the pioneer among all women conductors in America.

Long before the public had become accustomed to women in any profession, Miss Steiner was forging a successful career for herself as orchestra leader and composer. The daughter of a distinguished American family, she was born in Baltimore, Md. in 1867 and showed exceptional talent at an early age. She was barely eleven years old, when she began the composition of the grand opera, *Animaida*, "conceded by musical authorities to have some merit." A year later she wrote a tenor solo, *I Envy the Rose*, "which was sung by artists both in America and Europe."

Beginning her public career as assistant musical director to Edward E. Rice and Collier's 'Iolanthe' Company, this versatile musician conducted, during a period of thirty years, over 6000 performances of light and grand opera in the United States and Canada. On December 9, 1894, she led in New York the famous Anton Seidl Orchestra of 80 musicians in a program of her own. She was also musical director for Heinrich Conried, shortly before the latter joined the Metropolitan Opera House. Incidentally, a biographical sketch about her quotes Conried as having told her that he would have appointed her conductor at the Metropolitan, if only he dared.

Her death in 1929 was caused partly by worry and strain incidental to the establishment of a Home for Aged Musicians at Bay Shore. L. I., a project which she had conceived and for which she had worked tirelessly but without much success since 1925.

"IS IT woman's or women's? I note that some of the groups call themselves by one term, the rest by the other. I contend that woman's is right. We once referred this question to august professors of English and they confirmed the point for us. It's always called a man's, not a men's, orchestra. On that basis, it should be a woman's, not a women's, Symphony," writes Mr. Herbert Whittaker, business manager of the Long Beach, California, Woman's Symphony Orchestra.

He Dared!

The system of 'mixed' symphonic bodies in America was given one of its first tests toward the end of the gay nineties when John Lund, conductor of the Buffalo Orchestra, included among his first violin players a Nora Clench, who stayed with the ensemble over a number of years and "fiddled successfully with the best of her colleagues".

Here and There

Alfred Wallenstein, who, before he became a radio celebrity, served as first cellist with the Chicago Symphony and later with the New York Philharmonic, will appear in Chicago on February 16 as soloist and guest-conductor with the Woman's Symphony Orchestra

* * *

A fund-raising campaign for the benefit of the New York Women's Symphony has been launched by the group's Board of Directors. The Orchestra gives its next concert on February 23 in Carnegie Hall under the baton of Antonia Brico.

* * *

Consistently preferring to be led by a man, the Los Angeles Women's Symphony, is now under the direction of Wm. Ulrich, the fourth maestro to preside over this group of 70 players since its inception back in the fall of 1893.

* * *

A string ensemble of eight girl students from the Juilliard Graduate School participated at the reception-concert given at the Cosmopolitan Club on Sunday night, January 31, in honor of George Enesco, by the League of Composers. The octette has been trained by Mr. Hans Letz.

* * *

Under the auspices of the New York Flute Club, a quintet trained by Mr. Georges Barrere and comprising Lorna Wren, flute, Lois Wann, oboe, Ellen Stone, horn, Erika Kutzing, bassoon and Beatrice Merlau, clarinet, gave its first concert in the Beethoven Association's Clubhouse on Sunday, January 31st.

* * *

When last heard from, the Women's Symphony of Pittsburgh was "coming along very nicely indeed", according to Carl Simonis, its leader.

* * *

The Federal Symphony, a WPA project in New York, which employs 100 musicians, has Carmelita Ippolito as its Concertmaster.

ALL IS QUIET AGAIN ON SOUTHERN FRONT

Baltimore, Md. Jan. 31—A discord in local music circles preceded the first appearance which a group of women string instrumentalists made yesterday, as players of the twenty-year-old municipal Baltimore Symphony where feminine membership in the past was limited to the harp section only. The disagreement started about ten days ago, soon after Mr. Frederick R. Huber, civic director of music, appointed five women in the orchestra's violin, viola and cello choirs.

Three of Mr. Huber's appointees, being members of the Baltimore Musical Union, joined the orchestra without causing any discord. Trouble started, however, when the two others, after applying for their Union cards, found out that even if they would be accepted as members of the Local, they would still be denied the right to play with the orchestra this season.

The situation created by the Union's ruling stirred up lively controversies between Mr. Huber, who charged sex discrimination and Mr. Apple, the Local's President, who stated that "every Union has the inherent right to deny membership to any male or female, if they desire to gain admission to the organization for the sole purpose of displacing its regularly employed members, which is the only contention in this controversy, and not a question of sex."

As a result of this discord, the members in the orchestra threatened four days ago to walk out, in defense of Union rights, and quit their posts for the rest of the season. Finally, Mr. Huber named as substitutes for the excluded pair, two union women musicians who played with the three others in yesterday's concert under the baton of Ernest Shelling.

NEW YORK CITY—A not so frequent role of soloist, as far as women instrumentalists are concerned, will be undertaken on Monday night, February 15, when, in the course of its Carnegie Chamber concert, the Orchestrette Classique will present Helen Enser, player of the French Horn, as the assisting artist in Mozart's Concerto No. 3 in E. Flat Major. Frederique Petrides is the conductor of this group, which consists principally of young players and is now in its fourth season.

Published by the "Orchestrette Classique", 190 East End Ave., New York City.

Spanish born **José Iturbi** (1895–1980) was trained as a pianist and conductor at the Valencia Conservatory and the Paris Conservatoire. In 1929, he came to the United States and in 1930 went on an American tour. His first appearance in films began when his fingers impersonated Chopin's in *A Song to Remember.* Iturbi had a large popular following.

A few hours after his statement concerning women in music reached delighted editors' desks, the revolution began. That he would have made such a statement is astounding since his sister Amparo (1898–1969) was a pianist and often performed with him.

In coming to the defense of "the women," Spencer B. Driggs, writing an editorial column in the *Musical Advance* (vol. 25, no. 4–5, April 1937), used Petrides as an example of ability.

> In addition to the Woman's Symphony Orchestra [conducted by Brico], New York is fortunate in having another organization known as Orchestrette Classique—a Woman's Miniature Symphony Orchestra under the direction of Frédérique Petrides. This is an organization for Mr. Iturbi to take note of. Composed of ten first and second violins, two violas, two celli, two double basses, two flutes, oboe, three clarinets, two bassoons, two French horns, tympani and piano, the combination is extremely colorful. A recent performance at Carnegie Chamber Hall attracted no little attention and the program contained the Bach Symphony in D major, Grieg Holberg Suite, Mozart Concerto for French Horn in E flat major, Haydn Symphony No. 4 in D major and Sibelius Rakastava Suite for Strings and Tympani. There was no question of the ability of these musicians. The performance was interesting and delightful. It might be a profitable suggestion for the conductors of these orchestras to go a step further and give a few programs on which only works by women composers are played. That might be a novelty. There are probably many works which have never had a hearing and women like Eleanor Everest Freer have long had visions of symphonic works which until now would hardly be considered by conductors.

News, Facts, Activities	# WOMEN IN MUSIC	No Crusading; No Pleading

Vol. II. No. 6 — *Edited by Frederique Petrides* — MARCH, 1937

An Outbreak and a Prophecy

"I don't know how many days are left for Iturbi, but he surely has let himself in for a lot of trouble," said Mr. Leonard Liebling on February 4,—the day after the Spanish artist's much talked about interview on women in music and in sports appeared in the Toronto "Press".

According to the interview in the Canadian newspaper, Mr. Iturbi said that women can never achieve greatness in music and in sports. He is glad to have them play and sing of course, "because it gives them a change from their domestic life." However, "their efforts while praiseworthy and occasionally reaching artistry, never achieve greatness." Why? Simply because the Señor believes that "women are physically limited from attaining the standard of men and are limited temperamentally besides."

As was to be expected, Iturbi's outbreak (branded as "injudicious" in the "New York Sun" by Dr. William J. Henderson, dean of American critics) was "zealously noted down by the malicious press and broadcast to the world." It stirred up quite a storm, although various persons believed and still assert that either the Señor has been misquoted by the Toronto newspaper or he had merely tried to amuse himself and his readers by giving a provocative newspaper story.

Aux Armes, Musiciens! Marchons!

Among the first to answer the pianist-conductor was Antonia Brico, who, after defending the ability of members of her sex to attain eminence in music and in sports defied "Mr. Iturbi or any other symphony orchestra leader to bring a group of his men musicians and try them out in competition with a group of women musicians, the judges to be blindfolded and to decide on ability alone."

The challenge for a blindfold test was warmly upheld by Dorothy Dunbar Bromley, who wrote in her column on Feb. 9: "The Philharmonic Symphony, like many others, is an exclusive masculine preserve, and yet, it hardy seems possible that there would not be a certain number of women as good as the 105 men who play for the Society. If there aren't, I don't see why the good music schools take their money."

A "War of the Sexes"

As far as can be ascertained, the only public defence of Iturbi's thesis, appeared in the editorial page of "The New York Times". Thus, a paragraph in "Topics of the Times" (Feb. 6) stated: "Yet he (Iturbi) said no more than physicians, anthropologists and psychologists have been saying these many years—saying no more than that men and women are physically and temperamentally different and that these differences account for man's supremacy in art and sport." However, on the day when "The

IN THE YEAR 2037 A. D.

St. Peter:—Nothing doing! This Iturbi of yours must go to Purgatory first!

St. Gabriel:—Oh, come on and let the fellow in! Why back in 1937 he went through more than mere Purgatory! Have you forgotten his Toronto interview?

Times" printed the above quoted paragraph, an editorial in the "New York World-Telegram" asserted under the heading "WAR OF THE SEXES" that "to deny women musical stature is a fighting challenge" and that once one "gets them really stirred up" women "can be about anything they wish. That includes greatness, too."

Thank You Señor, Thank You!

On the other hand, "Musical Courier" handled the issue with amused interest. A playful although very diplomatic editorial in its February 20 number, stated that Iturbi spoke "no doubt in an unguarded moment" and it proceeded to report a "much hornet-like zooming in the feministic camps, the cohorts of which are even now considering an assault on the Spanish musician's penthouse."

However, the editorial, which ended by suggesting the hoisting of the "olive branch" and the declaration of "armistice", featured a letter written by a Mme Jackowska, who wrote:" We must thank Iturbi for giving us the opportunity which we have sought for so long, to open a real campaign, a fair campaign, to prove to the skeptical like himself, that women when they have been given the opportunity and possibility of devoting themselves from their childhood to the art or career they love, attain greatness and power as well as beauty in art, sciences, letters, sports or any other career."

The Truth of the Matter

On the day when the "Courier" printed its own neither-here-nor-there comments on "the burning question, Are Women Musicians Inferior to Males?", out in Los Angeles, the "Pacific Coast Musician" was stating editorially: "The men greatly outnumber the women as superlative artists. Yet, there are not a few women instrumentalists quite able to justify a claim to greatness, women probably unexcelled by the best male artists. (There appears to be an almost universal prejudice against giving the superlative woman artist her due. The average critic must qualify her one of the greatest 'women artists.')

"It should not be forgotten that women were given no chance till relatively recent times to show whether they could bring forth a Bach or Beethoven. And no Mozart or Haydn has been produced by the men since the day the way was opened to women to develop their gifts as those masters developed theirs."

Issue and Effects

By the end of February the women were "still up in arms at Jose Iturbi's . . . . uncontradicted statement which will have a far reaching effect," according to an item in "Musical Leader" (Chicago, Feb. 27) which questioned the wisdom of Mr. Iturbi's remarks and stated: women "may not have the physical power to punish the piano but artistically their standard is no lower than that of the gallant sex to which Mr. Iturbi belongs."

A Different Era, Mr. Iturbi!

Regardless whether Mr. Iturbi spoke seriously or otherwise in the course of his "injudicious outbreak" in Toronto, he added no strength, no new wings to the crippled and anaemic cause of a musical status quo among the sexes. Because the world denied women musical genius or ability in the bad old days, there is no reason for denying it to them now and in the future.

"No Crusading; No Pleading"

As a result of the controversy stirred up by Mr. Iturbi's statements some readers are wondering if it would not be advisable for "Women in Music" to adopt in the future a militant policy instead of adhering to its tactics of "no crusading, no pleading." Inasmuch as 'Women in Music' is sponsored by a group of young artists who feel that there is no better and more effective way for women conductors and orchestra players to further their professional cause than through the merits of their work, and that alone, there will be no change in policy.

And Lest You Forget

Hinde Barnett, concertmaster of the Orchestrette Classique, will be the soloist in the concert which this ensemble will give at Carnegie Chamber Music Hall on Monday night, April 26. She will render the Concerto in E Major by Johann Sebastian Bach. Frederique Petrides is the conductor.

Published by the "Orchestrette Classique", 190 East End Ave., New York City.

Early Orchestrette appearance, ca. 1935

The Orchestrette Classique. Courtesy Music Division, The New York Public Library.

| News, Facts, Activities | # WOMEN IN MUSIC | No Crusading No Pleading |

Edited by Frederique Petrides

Vol. II. No. 7   APRIL, 1937

"WIDELY MISQUOTED", JOSE ITURBI STATES

Expressing his "admiration for woman's accomplishments in various fields of endeavor," Senor Jose Iturbi, the pianist-conductor, in a letter recently published under his own signature in the *Rochester Journal*, claims that he has been "widely misquoted" in the famous interview which he gave in Toronto last February on women in music etc.

Parts of Mr. Iturbi's letter, reprinted in this column purely as a matter of record, read as follows:

"Recently I have been widely misquoted on a subject which is so important to me that it cannot be lightly dismissed. I refer to the Toronto interview...."

"I DID NOT say that 'women are inferior.' I DID say that 'women are, in certain fields, inferior to men.' I DID NOT say that 'women cannot be great and consequently cannot accomplish many wonderful things in life.' I DID say that 'women accomplish many wonderful things that I both respect and, admire, but they are limited by their natural endowments."

"I believe women play a very necessary part in life and that they can never be replaced by men. In some fields they cannot be equaled. I refer for example to the voice of Flagstad, the grace of Pavlowa, the art of Leonora Duse, etc."

After stating that "he cannot think of women who have accom--plished" (in history or in the present) "as great deeds" as some of the world's most illustrious men have accomplished in the arts, literature politics, etc., Señor Iturbi sees fit to voice "admiration" for such women as George Sand, Mrs. Stern, Landowska, Myra Hess, Amelia Earhart and Suzanne Lenglen. And he concludes:

"Summing it all up, I believe that women have a very definite and a very necessary place in life and I DO admire their accomplishments in various fields of endeavor."

SINCE by some sort of a diabolical coincidence(!) the bright boys and girls of the Fourth Estate appear to have been intent upon misquoting the bland Mr. Iturbi even before his Toronto interview, it would seem that, for revenge if nothing else, he should refrain in the future from using the press as the medium for enlightening the public on his views —unless he speaks in the presence of witnesses!

They Scoop!

The story of women's orchestras and women conductors will be told with illustrations in the course of an all-inclusive article on women musicians, which is scheduled for publication in the April 30th issue of the *Family Circle*, a weekly popular magazine with a 1,509,000 circulation in the South, the Mid-West and the Pacific Coast. This will be the first time that the subject of orchestras and conductors on the distaff side will be presented in the pages of a magazine outside the musical profession. The article is written by Mr. Stewart Robertson.

Shop Talk

With the world talking of the impending Coronation in England, this column cannot help remembering that Queen Dowager Mary was among those who lent in the past their moral and financial support to the British Woman's Symphony Orchestra which was launched in London in 1924 as a retaliatory step against the exclusion of women instrumentalists from the Musicians' Union in that city.

* * *

The first and only Japanese girl-violinist to play in a Symphony Orchestra in America is included in the ranks of Eva Anderson's municipally supported Woman's Symphony in Long Beach, California.

* * *

Under the sponsorship of the American friends of Spanish Democracy, the Cleveland Women's Orchestra, Hymen Schandler conductor, gave a benefit concert for the establishment of an American medical unit for the Loyalist cause in Spain.

* * *

About 100 players and 250 mixed voices participated in the program with which the New York Women's Symphony, Antonio Brico conductor, ended its third season on March 30th.

* * *

Baltimore, Philadelphia, Long Beach and Chicago, have also heard concerts given recently by their local feminine orchestras.

* * *

Helen Enser whose solo work in Mozart's Third Concerto for French horn and orchestra earned the warm praise of critics who heard her at the Orchestrette concert, (Feb. 15), repeated the same piece at a performance of the Federal Music Project Chamber Orchestra (New York) as a guest artist, on April 9, under the conductorship of Albert Stoessel.

ORCHESTRETTE ENDS ITS FOURTH SEASON

New York City.—The axiom that many things can be accomplished, provided a group settles down to sustained effort, also applies in the case of the Orchestrette Classique,— a small symphonic body of young musicians which, formed at the peak of the depression with a nucleus of six players, will give the final concert of its fourth season on Monday night, April 26, at Carnegie Chamber Hall.

Ever since its inception, this group of 28 players has aspired to perfect itself as an orchestra, to build up a worth-while repertoire and to develop a steady following among all classes of concert-goers. Self-managed and functioning without any éclats of publicity, it has succeeded in gradually establishing ambitious standards for its concerts; in widening the circle of those who are familiar with its work and in always netting definite earnings to its players

Proud of its own players, the Orchestrette always draws its soloists from artists in the fold. Two of these, Hinda Barnett, concertmaster, and Lois Wann, oboist, are featured as assisting artists for its April 26th concert. They will appear in a program, which, besides presenting compositions by Johann Sebastian Bach and by Mozart, father and son, will offer works by Henry Holden Huss and Arthur Foote, veteran American composers, and will usher in the first performance of an "Episodic Suite" for Small Orchestra, composed by Julia Smith, the ensemble's pianist since 1933, whose two previous orchestral works were also given their premieres by the group. Incidentally, the first of Miss Smith's works was played in 1935; the other in February, 1936.

IT SEEMS that the only woman conductor, who knows just how it feels to be confronted with a sit-down strike in an orchestra, is the Viennese Carmen Studer Weingartner. More than two years ago, and as previously reported here, Madame Weingartner was to direct a rehearsal of the Vienna Philharmonic. But the men in the orchestra did not like the idea of taking directions from a woman. Claiming that their parts were so full of mistakes that they could not go on, those ingenuous wretches remained on their seats but refused to give her the desired rehearsal.

Published by the "Orchestrette Classique", 190 East End Ave., New York City.

VOL. II, NO. 8, JUNE 1937

Texas-born **Olga Samaroff** (née Hickenlooper, 1880?–1948), pianist and teacher, was the first American woman to win a scholarship to the Paris Conservatoire. Trained by her grandmother and mother, she made her New York debut in 1905 and enjoyed an international reputation as a pianist, appearing with major orchestras. Samaroff was a charter faculty member of the Juilliard graduate school and piano department chairman at the Philadelphia Conservatory. Her pupils included Eugene List, Rosalyn Tureck, and Alexis Weissenberg. She founded the Schubert Memorial to aid young American musicians and published several books. Samaroff was married to Stokowski from 1911 to 1923 (McGillen and McGillen).

It should be noted that the *New Grove Dictionary of American Music* gives Samaroff's birth date as 1882.

The **National Federation of Music Clubs** represents about five thousand organizations in the United States and Puerto Rico. It was founded in Springfield, Illinois, in 1898 to "foster cooperation among people and organizations in the furthering of musical education; to integrate music into civic, educational, and social life; to stimulate American composition; and to promote American performers."

Each year since 1924, it has designated a week in May as National Music Week and since 1955 has encouraged the performance of American composition through a program called the Parade of American Music. The organization gives many awards to young artists and gives an annual award of one thousand dollars to foreign musical organizations to encourage the performance of American music abroad.

The **Berlin Women's Orchestra** was conducted by **Elizabeth Kuyper** (*Women in Music,* November 1936). Women in German orchestras still remain a rarity. In 1982 Judith Somogi (1943–88) auditioned for and received an appointment as conductor of the Frankfurt Opera. The importance of this appointment can be understood only when one realizes the Berlin Opera shattered tradition the same year by hiring its first woman violinist.

Mathilde Ernestine corresponded with Petrides and also visited her while in New York on her way to Paris. She pledged to carry information concerning Petrides and her work to Paris and the exposition. At this time, Ernestine was an editor and an officer in the League of American Pen Women and worked for Elena Moneak who was the director of the

News, Facts, Activities	# WOMEN IN MUSIC	No Crusading; No Pleading

Vol. II. No. 8   *Edited by Frederique Petrides*   JUNE, 1937

URGES EDUCATION, NOT THE WARPATH

The question of women in music was discussed extensively at the Music Clubs' Convention in Indianapolis (April 26) by Madame Olga Samaroff, pianist, authoress and educator, who, after outlining the causes behind "the baseless discrimination" against women in certain fields of music, suggested education rather than "going on the warpath" to end existing prejudices and challenged the Federation to give and help establish equal opportunities in fees and engagements between gifted men and female solo instrumentalists, orchestral conductors and players.

Madame Samaroff mentioned her shock when as a young concert pianist in 1908, she was told by her manager that he was able to get her many engagements because she was a woman and therefore "booked" at smaller fees than men pianists of equal rank. "Then I understood", she added, "that the discrimination against women in music begins when they enter into direct competition with men."

"The real reason....why women musicians still have such a hard time entering the ranks of most major symphony orchestras, why women orchestral conductors are frowned upon or ridiculed and are never to be found even among the guest conductors of such organizations is purely economic," she continued in the course of her forceful analysis.

"In the past women have often been more hostile to movements designed for their own benefit than men," but, "if the hundreds of thousands of women who compose the National Federation of Music Clubs approach the question of 'Women in Music' with wisdom, art itself will benefit," were some of Madame Samaroff's concluding remarks.

THEY say that quite a few musicians like nothing better than to ignore each other when engaged in similar activities and yet, in the printed program for its special concert in Mt. Lebanon, Pa. on June 3, the Women's Symphony of Pittsburgh will present an outline of the aims of other kindred feminine ensembles in America. The sketch has been prepared by the Orchestrette Classique at the suggestion of Mr. Carl Simonis, conductor of the Pittsburgh group.

Verdi's Predicament

Only on exceptional occasions does the Roman Catholic Church in Europe allow women to sing in her services. Thus, writing in the year 1868, Verdi says: "If I were in the good graces of St. Peter, I would beg him to be kind enough to allow, at least, for this once only, that women should take part in the performance of this Mass; but as I am not, it will be necessary to find some one more suitable than myself to attain this end." The Mass in question was the one written by a group of composers in memory of Rossini.

Shop Talk

The Berlin Women's Orchestra, composed of fourteen players, gave a concert recently in Florence, Italy.

* * *

A great deal of its unprecedented financial success throughout the season just expired is attributed by the Woman's Symphony of Chicago to the wonderful support of local women's clubs. For instance: Mrs. Adolf Hoffman, State Music Chairman, and her leaders in various districts bought tickets in quantities, gave contributions to the orchestra's various funds and spread the news of its activities wherever they spoke in public.

* * *

In the jargon of "swing" musicians, a violinist is a "squeaker", a critic is "the boogie man" and a symphony player is a "long hair".

* * *

The mixed orchestra as a reality in the future was explained by Frederique Petrides, on May 24, to the boy and girl-students who play in the 100-piece orchestra of the High School of Music and Art, New York. After her talk, the speaker led this training ensemble in Schubert's Unfinished Symphony.

* * *

While in Europe this summer, Miss Mathilde Ernestine, Director of the Beaux Arts Salon, 505 N. Michigan Avenue, Chicago, Ill., will make a survey of women on the dais and in orchestras in major cities of England, France, Belgium and Holland which she will visit with members of the American Good-Will Tour to the Paris Exposition of 1937. This is a Tour for musicians, writers and art-lovers, scheduled to sail under her leadership on July 9th from New York on the "Isle de France", and return on August 11th.

WPA WOMEN'S UNIT HAILED AS ASSET

Boston, Mass.—Fifty-two musical Eves, some of whom belonged to the Fadettes Orchestra around 1915, comprise the Commonwealth Women's Symphony, which was launched in this city last September and is the only symphonic unit of the WPA Federal Music Project to employ feminine musicians exclusively. As for Adam, he, too, is represented in the group in the person of Mr. Solomon Branslavsky, its conductor, who has led successfully the forty concerts which this ensemble has to its credit since its inception.

In the beginning, the "Commonwealth" presented concerts mostly as a part of the curriculum in the various high and grammar schools. During the past few months, however, it has been included in the list of WPA units to be booked on a paying basis. This procedure creates "a most encouraging reaction, even to the extent of having return engagements for the Orchestra," to quote Mr. Wm. Haddon, State Supervisor of the Federal Music Project, who, commenting on the record established thus far by this aggregation, expressed himself as follows to *Women in Music*: "We have received nothing but the highest praise for the work of this unit. Everyone considers it one of the finest efforts of the Federal Music Project."

(Ed. Note: Women's orchestras are not a novelty in the musical history of Boston, where Caroline Nichols, a violin orchestral player, organized in 1889 the Fadettes Women's Orchestra. This group was to blossom out some few years later as the first pretentious and famous venture of professional women musicians in the United States. By 1910, its work was known from Coast to Coast).

Besides including 2253 feminine musicians in its rolls as of April 1, 1937, the Federal Music Project, according to WPA headquarters in Washington, D. C., has also featured as guest conductors with some of its major symphony orchestras the following: Antonia Brico (Brooklyn Symphony), Ebba Sundstrom (Philadelphia Civic), Elizabeth Woodson (Virginia Symphony), Lela Hanmer (Illinois Symphony) and Henriette Schumann (Syracuse Symphony Orchestra).

Published by the "Orchestrette Classique", 190 East End Ave., New York City.

Medinah Club in Chicago. This no doubt is the same Moneak who founded and conducted the Chicago Women's Symphony in 1925. The letterhead on Ernestine's correspondence carried the names of the club's patrons; Eleanor Freer was among those listed.

The brochure for the exposition tour describes the tour director as Mlle. Ernestine, director of the Beaux Arts Salon at the Medinah Club of Chicago, "which presents a 'New Star Series of American Artists' each Sunday at 4:00."

The American Good Will Tour sailed July 9 on the *SS Isle De France* and returned August 11 on the *SS Normandie*. There were French lessons aboard, and the group was limited to twenty-five. (New York–to–New York fare in third class was $485, tourist $585, cabin $855.)

The **Federal Music Project** was part of the **Works Progress Administration (WPA)**, which was a program initiated in 1935 by President Franklin D. Roosevelt. The main purpose was to aid composers and performers during the Depression by providing work for unemployed musicians. The program was suspended in 1941.

| News, Facts, Activities | # WOMEN IN MUSIC | No Crusading; No Pleading |

Vol. III. No. 1   *Edited by Frederique Petrides*   July, 1937

"NO GOOD REASON" FOR BAN ON WOMEN

Like a good many other American writers on music and musicians, William J. Henderson, the Dean of New York music critics, who died last month, was in favor of including women in orchestras. His authoritative voice was raised more than once in behalf of women as conductors and orchestral players. The following comments on the subject were printed in his New York *Sun* column on Saturday, November 16, 1935. Quoted in parts, they read:

"There is no good reason why women should not be employed in orchestras. The chief question to be asked is whether they can play as well as men. After that, other considerations may be taken up. Can a conductor enforce discipline among the women as well as he can among the men, or will they have recourse to the defence of tears when the hard-hearted one addresses the instrumental body in merciless rebuke? Can women endure the severe strain of long and repeated rehearsals? That as well as other questions become individual rather than general. All a conductor needs to know is not whether women can fill all the requirements, but whether the particular woman can, whom he contemplated engaging.

"Are there female performers on all kinds of instruments? Certainly ... Now there must have been a fine spirit of enterprise in the soul of a woman who took up the study of the tympani. How many jobs are there for the female tympanist? What is the outlook for the female bassoonist? Does any one wish to see a woman playing the bass drum or an E flat tuba?...

"Well it is all a matter of custom. Students in such institutions as the Juilliard School of Music see women playing in their orchestra continually and think nothing of it...."

An orchestra of Japanese women, reputed to be the first one of its kind in Tokio, was playing at the Imperial Theatre of that city in 1925. However, the group was allowed to play only when actresses were on the stage. When actors appeared, another orchestra, composed of males, was there to take its place and provide the music.

Land of Sopranos

A European composer's observation that America "seems to be the natural home of the soprano," prompted Louis Elson to remark in his *History of American Music:* "No scientist has yet investigated the cause of national characteristics of voice. It may be climate, or food, or heredity that causes North Spain to bring forth tenors; Switzerland, male falsetto singers ('joddlers'); England, contraltos; Russia, basses; and America, sopranos."

Shop Talk

This number inaugurates the third volume of *Women in Music.* With two volumes to its credit on a little known and never classified or coordinated subject-matter, the publication is the first to ever attempt a factual survey—historical and current—of activities of symphony conductors and orchestras on the distaff side.

* * *

Most of the facts printed in *Women in Music* have been collected through research work and correspondence with groups and individuals.

* * *

Ruth Kemper officiated as guest-conductor at the concert given by the Commonwealth Women's Orchestra of Boston (WPA) on June 30 in Hudson, Mass.

* * *

Lela Hanmer is the conductor of the Woods Symphony Orchestra, a mixed amateur orchestra in Western Springs, Illinois. She is a professional musician.

* * *

Among the players employed this summer in Nino Marcelli's San Diego Symphony, a mixed orchestra, are Lois Wann, oboist, and Virginia Payton, cellist, both of whom are residents of New York City.

* * *

Two of the three winners at a musical contest for school children held in Central Park, on June 19, under the auspices of the Department of Parks of the City of New York, were girls. Frederique Petrides, conductor of the Orchestrette Classique, was one of the judges.

* * *

"Why should we not have women conductors and orchestras? Why should not women play orchestral instruments?" Wm. Henderson, *Sun,* March 14, 1932.

AMERICA APPLAUDED PIONEER'S WORK

Boston, Mass.—Caroline B. Nichols, who, for over a quarter of a century, has trained more young women musicians for professional, wage earning and self-supporting orchestra jobs than any other individual, in America, lives now a quiet, peaceful life in this city, where she first achieved fame in the 'nineties as the founder and conductor of the celebrated Fadette Women's Orchestra of Boston.

Formed here in 1888 and active up to 1920, Mrs. Nichols' concert group was nationally hailed as one of the first competent women's orchestras in this country. Throughout its existence, it gave no less than 6063 concerts in Lyceum courses in the United States and Canada, in concert halls, parks and summer resorts and also, as "headliner", in first class vaudeville houses from Coast to Coast. These activities yielded over $500,000 to the more than 600 women on its payroll at one time or another

Critics, writers, musicians and audiences everywhere were favorably impressed by the work of the Fadettes, as the group was popularly known. Its repertory included symphonies, all the classical overtures, seventy-five grand operas, numerous salon pieces and popular selections.

While still in its formative days, Mrs. Nichols' orchestra was "aided and abetted" by her brother-in-law, Mr. George H. Chickering (President of the Chickering Piano Co.) and gave recitals in Chickering Hall, besides playing at social functions and large meetings. Named after the heroine in George Sands' classic "La Petite Fadette," it was started with six players, but gradually added new units. Around 1896, there were some twenty musicians in its string, brass, wood and percussion sections.

The Fadette Orchestra took its initial step toward widespread fame in 1898. Four years later, in 1902, it started off as a major attraction on the Keith Circuit and for about fifteen years toured each winter from Coast to Coast, returning in the summer to Keith's Boston House as an augmented ensemble of forty players.

Retired now, Caroline B. Nichols is still remembered with affection and admiration as a fine leader on and off the conductor's podium.

Stockton, California, has also a women's orchestra now. It is under the direction of Virginia L. Short.

Published by the "Orchestrette Classique", 190 East End Ave., New York City.

VOL. III, NO. 2, SEPTEMBER 1937

Albert Roussel was born in 1869. The string sinfonietta referred to was probably one of his last works, since he died August 23, 1937.

Ebba Sundstrom did not return to the Chicago Woman's Symphony after this leave of absence.

In March 1940 **Herliczka** and **Scheerer** each gave a Town Hall concert within the same week. This event was covered in the *New Yorker* (March 30, 1940) under a heading of "Ladies Who Lead."

> The two maestre made an interesting contrast. Miss Herliczka led her band without a score or baton, Miss Scheerer used music and stick. Miss Herliczka's technique was unconventional, Miss Scheerer's was more traditional. Miss Herliczka's program consisted largely of relatively unfamiliar items; Miss Scheerer's offerings, which were fewer in number . . . included real strangers. Both ladies had great energy and an obvious grasp of the music they conducted.

Virginia Short corresponded with Petrides on stationery with a letterhead that read:

> Music Department
> Stockton High School
> Frank Thornton Smith, Head of Department—Vocal
> Virginia L. Short, Orchestras—Theory
> Harold A. Heisinger, Bands

In her letters, Short gave many details of her organization and commented on how loyal and interesting her players were in spite of not all being excellent musicians. She expressed a longing for conducting engagements other than a school orchestra. In October 1937 Short wrote that Antonia Brico had been in California and would be conducting WPA Orchestra concerts in San Francisco and Oakland.

The **Chicago Women's Concert Band** was founded and conducted by **Lillian Poenisch**, first clarinetist and "one of the founders" of the the Chicago Woman's Symphony. Born in Cheney, Kansas, Poenisch studied clarinet and conducting with several teachers in the Chicago area and eventually taught at the American Conservatory of Music.

News, Facts, Activities

WOMEN IN MUSIC

No Crusading; No Pleading

Vol. III. No. 2   *Edited by Frederique Petrides*   September, 1937

WHEN THE FADETTES WERE THE VOGUE . . .

In view of the fact that printed anecdotes on women's orchestras, or on women conductors are among the world's greatest rarities, *Women in Music* offers its readers the following anecdotes from the records of the Fadettes Orchestra of Boston:

During an engagement at one of the annual Food Fairs at the Mechanics Building, Boston, an old gentleman who stood near the concert platform listening to the music as played by the Fadettes, stepped up to the leader and said: "Do you girls ever play in church?" "Oh, yes, sir," answered Caroline B. Nichols, the conductor-founder of the Fadettes.—"Well," said he, "I'd like to hire the orchestra to come to our town and play for our praise meetin'. Kin you play the "Hymn of Joy and Praise?"

Having been assured that the girls could play hymns all right, the inquiring gentleman told the leader that she would hear from him again and walked away, remarking to a companion: "Guess they'll ketch the sinners' fancy and give the minister some show."

The High School Association of Camden, Maine, engaged the Fadettes for Graduation exercises. When the Maine-bound musicians had embarked on a steamer of the Bangor S. S. Line, they met with a problem: only small instruments were allowed in the staterooms. As the bass player would not let the instrument out of her care, the negro porter on duty took hold of the "bull fiddle" by the neck. It so happened, however, that he was a stutterer, as also was the player. Each of the contestants tried vainly to protest and each thought that the other was trying to make fun of him or her. Finally the leader solved the impasse by explaining to each the speech defect of the other, whereupon the porter relented and let his fellow-stutterer have her way.

New York.—A cash prize of $500 for an original orchestral work will be awarded to the winner of the contest which the New York Women's Symphony Orchestra is conducting for the purpose of encouraging American composers. The work must be not less than ten nor more than twenty minutes in performance time. It will be played by the Orchestra, under Antonia Brico's baton, on March 15, at the organization's third concert of the forthcoming season.

An American!

The first great woman composer may turn out to be an American! Such is the opinion of Eva Mary Grew, the sholarly associate editor of the *British Musician* who believes that: "There is now admittedly more possibility of musical genius arising in women than ever before, and it may be in America that the first great master, or, if you will, mistress of music will appear."

Shop Talk

Gertrude Herliczka, the Viennese American, whose Town Hall concert is even now discussed very pleasantly by various Philharmonic Orchestra men who played under her command in 1935, is still in Europe. During the last two years she led symphony orchestras in France, Prague, Budapest, Vienna and Italy. On Dec. 29 she is to direct a concert of the famous "Societa Santa Cecilia" in Rome.

* * *

Phil Spitalny's all-girl jazz band is scoring triumph after triumph. Not only has it become one of radio's outstanding orchestras, but last month it filled a prolonged engagement at the New York Paramount Theatre. The orchestra, combined with the film "Artists and Models" drew capacity audiences and its original two-week engagement was extended to four weeks.

* * *

Conductor Jane Evrard whose seven-year-old orchestra of Parisian women is heard frequently in the French Capital, may well be proud of a string sinfonietta dedicated to her by A. Roussel, the eminent French composer. This work will be among the compositions to be played by the Orchestrette Classique this winter under the direction of Frederique Petrides.

* * *

Again honoring its policy of sponsoring conductorial talent among its own ranks, the Woman's Symphony of Chicago has put Gladys Welge, its assistant conductor, in full charge of its concert for December. Ebba Sundstrom, the group's conductor, enjoys now a one year's leave of absence.

* * *

About thirty women constitute the New York Chamber Orchestra which makes its debut in Town Hall on Oct. 12 under the direction of Jeannette Scheerer.

'SINFONETTA' FORMED BY STOCKTON WOMEN

Stockton, Cal.—Ever since the early nineties when San Francisco was the only city on the Pacific Coast to boast of a women's orchestra, various Californian communities have witnessed, at one time or another, the launching of similar aggregations within their gates. It was only last year, however, that Stockton has been introduced for the first time to the novelty of having its own feminine unit. Known as the "Sinfonetta" this group is composed of twenty players. It was founded in the fall of 1936 by Virginia L. Short, under whose conductorship it gave three concerts between last December and April 1937.

Miss Short is an enthusiastic and earnest musician who has studied conducting at the Mozarteum Academy in Salzburg. The community seems to be genuinely interested in her "Sinfonetta," which functions as yet without financial backing. She plans three and possibly four concerts next season, offering unfamiliar and choice music.

The "Sinfonetta" does not infringe on the territory of the Stockton Symphony Orchestra. Composed at present of string players only, it contemplates a gradual addition of brass and wind instruments but does not intend to ever outgrow its chamber orchestra complexion.

Two sets of mother and daughter play in this group, which is composed principally of young players, and which rehearses regularly in a hall provided by the Stockton High School.

(Other current orchestras of women in California are: the Long Beach Women's Symphony Orchestra, which was founded in 1925 and functions under the conductorship of Eva Anderson, a Howard Hanson pupil; and the Los Angeles Women's Symphony, founded in 1893, conducted by Mr. William Ulrich.)

Chicago, Ill.—A new organization, the Chicago Women's Concert Band, was heard this summer in the course of the municipally sponsored concerts on Navy Pier. Lillian Poenisch, first clarinetist and one of the founders of the local Women's Symphony, is the conductor of the group which was organized last year and is said to be the only entirely feminine band of professional musicians in this country. Instrumental solos by members of the band were featured.

Published by the "Orchestrette Classique", 190 East End Ave., New York City.

VOL. III, NO. 3, OCTOBER 15, 1937

Pianist **Anne (or Anna) Mehlig Falk** was born in Stuttgart in 1843 (this date varies depending on the source) and died in Berlin in 1928. She made her debut in England in 1866 and successfully toured Europe and the United States. Mehlig made two appearances with the New York Philharmonic in 1869 (Thompson, 1316).

Petrides corresponded with **George Schaun**, who had asked to be put on the mailing list of *Women in Music*. He kept her informed of musical events in Baltimore. Schaun was not only complimentary about the Orchestrette but expressed amazement at the extent of her research while involved in so many other activities.

News, Facts, Activities

WOMEN IN MUSIC

No Crusading; No Pleading

Vol. III. No. 3   *Edited by Frederique Petrides*   October 15, 1937

MIXED ORCHESTRAS IN EARLIER DAYS

It was an American who challenged in 1914 the exaggerated claims of George Shapiro, an English conductor employing at that time twenty-five women string players in his Symphony Orchestra in London, and who was, evidently, telling heaven and earth that "he was the first to recognize the artistic merits of women" as musicians.

This American, editor of the now defunct *New Music Review,* knew that there used to be a woman oboist in the Carl Rosa Opera Company sometime in the 'nineteen eighties. He also knew that the Moody-Manners Opera Company, which was formed in London in 1897, employed women in its orchestra. Moreover he remembered that 11 women string players were working in 1903 in Edouard Colonne's famous Symphony Orchestra in Paris. Consequently, he wrote and printed in his magazine an editorial, which shed some interesting light around the origin of the mixed orchestra in France and England, challenging thus Mr. Shapiro's claims for priority.

His editorial failed, however, to say anything regarding female players in early American Symphonies. And, were it not for an article written in 1909 by the late Maud Powell, the great American violinist, it seems that one would have to search far and wide, and probably in vain at that, for some data, no matter how flimsy, on the first steps toward mixed orchestras on this side of the ocean before the World War.

In the course of her article, Miss Powell spoke of the presence of women violin players in the Hartford Symphony Orchestra in 1909; also of Nora Clench, who played in the first violin section of the Buffalo Symphony in the late 'nineties. In addition, she extolled the "good sense of rhythm" as well as other traits that should qualify the American girl for orchestral work. Incidentally, her commendations antedated by almost seven years similar praises voiced by Leopold Stokowski, one of the few prominent American conductors to speak, more than twenty years ago, in favor of mixed orchestras.

Tennessee's own conductor, Bertha Clark, will be presented in the next issue of *Women in Music.*

Shop Talk

The news that the Boston Symphony has engaged Nadia Boulanger to conduct one of its February concerts, is in keeping with Boston's ever hospitable attitude toward women in music.

* * *

It was in Boston where the native girl is said to have made her "first efforts to express her musical ambitions" after 1776. It was there, too, that one of Liszt's pupils, Anne Mehlig, "the first really eminent woman pianist to come to America" and one of the earliest women to play here as orchestral soloist, made her debut in 1871 with the Theodore Thomas Symphony.

* * *

It was also in the "American Athens" where the first serious orchestra of native women was started in 1888 and it is there that the WPA Commonwealth Women's Orchestra functions now.

* * *

Besides being the first of her sex to lead the Boston Symphony, Miss Boulanger is also the only woman to ever be engaged, so far, as guest conductor by a major American Symphony Orchestra.

* * *

Girl wind instrumentalists seem to have fared quite well this year. For instance: so much was the San Diego Symphony pleased this summer with the work of Lois Wann, N. Y. oboist, that it has re-engaged her for next season. Also: Helen Enser, horn player, did good work as orchestral soloist, twice in New York (once under A. Stoessel) and three times in Westchester.

* * *

The two above-named players, among the first to join the Orchestrette about five years ago, have worked with it ever since. They will play at this group's next concert— the first of four during this season— on Monday night, November 8, at the Carnegie Chamber Hall, under Frederique Petrides. Hinda Barnett is their concertmaster in the Orchestrette Classique.

* * *

In a recent article on women's orchestras, the second from his pen since last January in the *Baltimore Sun,* Mr. George Schaun, music critic for that newspaper, pointed out to "strong evidence that the entry of women into orchestral music is no passing fad...."

MAJOR SYMPHONY IGNORES PRECEDENT

New York City.—With the disclosure, a few weeks ago, of an arrangement effected late this summer by the Pittsburgh Symphony Orchestra, interest among feminine musicians has naturally centered— not without ample and well-founded gratification, of course—on the inclusion in that symphonic body of a woman horn player.

The player is twenty-year old Ellen Stone, a native of Bogoda, N. J., and the first of her sex to ever be included in the brass section of a major symphonic body not composed exclusively of women. She was selected by Otto Klemperer, who held auditions this summer to choose ninety players for the Pittsburgh Symphony Orchestra.

Somewhat discouraged after two other tradition-steeped orchestras refused to employ her, despite her qualifications, this gifted artist was momentarily stunned to disbelief upon hearing that she was chosen as the Pittsburgh Orchestra's first horn, following her three auditions for Klemperer, who, by selecting a woman for this post, rose above precedent or discrimination between sexes in the orchestral field.

Miss Stone has received her ensemble training with the National Orchestra, at the Juilliard and Oberlin College. One of her many laurels is also the Philharmonic Scholarship for 1936-37, awarded her by the National Orchestral Ass'n. In view of the fact that horn players from her sex are given even less opportunities for orchestral engagements than their string-playing sisters in music, her Pittsburgh affiliation will, no doubt, prove an added incentive to women players of the horn, the oboe, bassoon, etc.

Full of faith now in a bright future for herself, Miss Stone expects to play in all thirty-six concerts of the Pittsburgh Symphony this season. Her arrangement provides her with a six-week term as the first horn. That term over, she will continue in that position, or she may be given the also important assignment as the third horn. In addition, she is to play the Strauss Concerto as the Symphony's soloist.

The new season finds no less than thirteen women's groups in America and about 700 players in the ranks.

Published by the "Orchestrette Classique", 190 East End Ave., New York City.

Sidney Lanier (1842–81) was a poet, flutist, and composer who was born in Macon, Georgia. He also wrote a number of books on music centering around the relationship of poetry and music. Some of his poetry was set by other composers and became well-known songs of the time. Petrides corresponded with Oliver Orr in Macon, Georgia, who used excerpts of Petrides's articles on Lanier in an editorial that appeared in the *Macon Telegraph*. At the time, there were active "Lanier Societies" and "Lanier Committees."

Otto Klemperer (1885–1973) was a German composer and conductor who spent part of his professional life in the United States. He became conductor of the Los Angeles Philharmonic (1933–39) and also conducted the New York Philharmonic, the Philadelphia Orchestra, and, in 1939, the Pittsburgh Symphony Orchestra. In 1939 he underwent surgery for a brain tumor and did little conducting for a number of years. In 1959 he became conductor of the Philharmonic Orchestra of London and remained there until his retirement from public concerts in 1972.

While Petrides had been informed that the **Saint Louis Women's Symphony** would give its first concert in the spring of 1937, a program states that February 27, 1939, was their first public performance. On Sunday, June 19, 1938, the *St. Louis Post-Dispatch* devoted a complete page to pictures of the group and the conductor, **Edith Gordon**. The accompanying article stated that

> Miss Edith Gordon, pianist for the St. Louis Symphony Chorus, tackled a man-size job when she accepted appointment as conductor of the newly organized 60 piece St. Louis Women's Symphony Orchestra. Recently she began rehearsing the musicians . . . who were carefully selected in a series of auditions held throughout the winter months.

News, Facts, Activities	WOMEN IN MUSIC	No Crusading; No Pleading

Vol. III. No.4   *Edited by Frederique Petrides*   December, 1937

FAMED NATIVE POET DISCERNED ABILITY

Sidney Lanier's advocacy of women in music is something not generally remembered or known in these days!

This is what the poet-flutist wrote sometime around 1876: "With the exception of the double bass and the heavier brass,—indeed I am not sure that these exceptions are necessary—there is no instrument in the orchestra which a woman cannot play successfully...The extent, depth and variety of musical capability among the women of the United States are continual new sources of astonishment and pleasure to this writer... There is no limit to the possible achievements of our countrywomen in this behalf if their efforts be once turned to the right direction. The direction is unquestionably the orchestra.

"All the world has learnt to play the piano. Let our young ladies —always saving of course those who have the gift for the special instrument—leave that and address themselves to the violin, the flute, the oboe, the harp, the clarinet, the bassoon. It is more than possible that upon some of these instruments the superior daintiness of the female tissue might finally make the woman a more successful player than the man.

"On the flute, for instance, a certain combination of delicacy with flexibility in the lips is absolutely necessary to bring out fully the passionate yet velvety tone hereinbefore alluded to; and many male players, of all requisite qualifications so far as manual execution is concerned, will be forever debarred from attaining it by reason of their intractable, rough note. The same, in less degree, may be said of the oboe and bassoon. Besides, the qualifications required are more often found in women than in men; for these qualifications are patience, fervor, and fidelity, combined with deftness of hand and intuiteveness of soul."—(Excerpts from "The Orchestra of To-Day", in *Scribner's*, April, 1880.)

Otto Klemperer has given more opportunities to women than any other first-rank conductor this year. Besides selecting a girl hornist for the Pittsburgh Symphony, he also has included two more women string players this season in the Los Angeles Symphony Orchestra.

Shop Talk

The opera season is on and just imagine anyone refusing these days to receive socially a Lotte Lehmann or a Flagstad because these great artists are opera singers! And yet, when in a burst of enthusiasm for music and for a great singer, John Ruskin, the famous English writer, begged his father to invite to their house the celebrated Jenny Lind, (1820-1887), the father refused the request on the grounds that "an opera singer did not belong to the sort of society" which could be received in a respectable home.

* * *

The newly-formed Saint Louis Women's Symphony Orchestra will hold its first concert in the spring. Edith Gordon, pianist and pupil of Rudolph Ganz, is the director. According to the *St. Louis Post Dispatch,* her orchestra was started "after the success of similar organizations in New York, Chicago and Philadelphia" and it will limit its membership to sixty players.

* * *

"Perhaps the day will come when men will be needed for orchestras only to subsidize them." The statement—not to be taken literally, of course,—was made by Mr. Oscar Thompson, a few weeks ago, in *The New York Sun.*

* * *

The very well-chosen program with which the New York Women's Symphony Orchestra opened its fourth season on November 30 included Handel's Concerto in G. Minor for strings and oboe. This beautiful concerto was rendered by Lois Wann, the only woman oboist to play it four times in New York, three times with the Orchestrette Classique since 1935, and this time under Miss Antonia Brico's direction.

* * *

Tickets for concerts make ideal Christmas gifts!

* * *

Melle. Boulanger of Paris who will offer Gabriel Fauré's *Requiem* as guest-conductor of the Boston Symphony in February, "proved a unique *maestra*", according to *The New Yorker,* in directing this composition at a Royal Philharmonic Society Concert (London) last month. "Her programme," to quote from the London *Times* of Nov. 5, "was a refreshing change from the conventional symphony concert so literally supplied to Londoners just now."

WILL PAY TRIBUTE TO LANIER'S VIEWS

New York City.—American women instrumentalists owe a debt of gratitude to the memory of Sidney Lanier, "Poet Laureate of the South", musician, critic and lecturer on English literature at Johns Hopkins University, who also played the first flute in Baltimore's Peabody Symphony Orchestra in the seventies.

Undoubtedly the first noted American in the last century to discern the merits of women as potential orchestral players, Lanier advocated with enthusiasm the studying by them of all orchestral instruments. This he did in his essay "The Orchestra of To-Day", which was written around 1876 and was originally published in *Scribner's* for April, 1880.

At the time the essay was published, the piano was the only accepted instrument for American women. Even the playing of the harp by one of them was something rare.

An idea of the stimulating influence exerted by the poet-flutist's advocacy was shown in an editorial in *Musical America* for April 28, 1906, which reads in part as follows:

"Sidney Lanier once declared that 'when our young women shall.... devote themselves...to the flute, the violin, the hautboy (oboe), the harp, the violoncello, the horn instruments ....' then will the women find a proper sphere in the world of instrumental music. Since Lanier made this comment, his suggestion has been taken up by many young women and the violin, violoncello and harp player is far more common than they were....' "

Lanier was born in Macon, Ga., on February 3, 1842. He died in Lynn, N. C., on September 7, 1881.

His advocacy of women for orchestras will be commemorated by the Orchestrette Classique, Frederique Petrides, conductor, with a concert on Monday evening, January 10, at the Carnegie Chamber Music Hall. Ruth Freeman, flutist, will be the soloist in Mozart's Concerto in D. Major.

Those juvenile globe-trotters— The Vienna Choir Boys—will be the soloists at the December 12 concert of the twelve-year-old Woman's Symphony of Chicago, the Orchestra which "contributes importantly to Chicago's artistic season", according to *Musical Leader.*

Published by the "Orchestrette Classique", 190 East End Ave., New York City.

VOL. III, NO. 5, JANUARY 1938

Russian born **Fabien Sevitzky** (1891–1967) became a naturalized citizen in 1928. He shortened his name from Koussevitzky to avoid confusion with Serge Koussevitzky. His tenure with the Indianapolis Symphony Orchestra lasted from 1937 to 1955.

Bertha Roth Walburn Clark (1882–1974) was born in Ohio and graduated from the Cincinnati College of Music in 1902 as an accomplished violinist. She and her first husband, Jamie Walburn, moved to Knoxville about 1910. She taught violin and voice, coached a local opera group, and founded a Ladies String Quartet. In 1923 she founded a Philharmonic Orchestra, which failed for a lack of funding. After Walburn's death, she met and married Harold Clark, a flutist and cellist. In 1925 she founded the Walburn-Clark Little Symphony, an ensemble of twenty-five members which was renamed the Knoxville Symphony Orchestra in 1927. The orchestra was officially chartered by the state of Tennessee in 1935, and Bertha Clark, still its conductor, began to be paid for her services. She retired as the orchestra's conductor in 1946, although she and her husband continued to play with the orchestra until 1962 (Ammer, 211–12).

Hungarian **Erno Rapee** (1891–1945) was best known for his arrangements for silent films and scores for sound films. He was general music director for Warner Brothers in California and later held the same position for NBC. He was appointed music director of Radio City Music Hall in New York in 1932—a position he held until his death.

| News, Facts, Activities | # WOMEN IN MUSIC | No Crusading; No Pleading |

Vol. III. No. 5   *Edited by Frederique Petrides*   January, 1938

THEY DID NOT FEEL FREE TO SWEAR!

Before women won their honorable place in every-day journalism, one of the stock arguments advanced against admitting them into the ranks of the working press was that the presence of "petticoat" newswriters in an editorial room would rob editors and others of their freedom of expression during office hours.

A similar concern for "freedom of expression" appears to have prevented many conductors in the past from including women in their organizations. Witness, for instance, what Mr. Richard Czerwonky, the Chicago conductor, had to say on the subject in the April 1923 issue of the now-defunct *Musical Observer*.

"Women orchestra players are not popular with conductors, mainly because the conductors do not feel at liberty to swear as occasion demands before them, as they do before a lot of men.

"A conductor, in the stress of rehearsal, cannot stop and delete his favorite remarks when things are not going so well, just because there are ladies present," the indiscreet Chicagoan continued. "He must have freedom of expression so that his players know just what he wants. No beating around the bush then. Time is too valuable. No man who is a gentleman can do this without the instinct of apology when there are women around—and that is the main reason why women are not popular as members of symphony orchestras."

Mr. Czerwonky's words are very illuminating, indeed. But something should also be said here about those baton wielders in the past, who had, it seems, the habit of telling Rabelaisian stories during rehearsals, no doubt in order to help the boys relax! The habit must have constituted another phase of conductorial rights to freedom of expression during rehearsals...

The New York Women's Symphony gives its next concert on Tuesday evening, Jan. 18, in Carnegie Hall.

"Lanier ought to be alive to-day. There are now more than a dozen symphonic ensembles (of women) in America," stated last month, *Diatonics*, that breezy music column in the *N. Y. World-Telegram*.—(The oldest of these orchestras is the one in Los Angeles. It was organized in 1893 by Professor H. Hamilton.),

Shop Talk

One of the first instances of women belonging to a musicians' union is that of the eight jugglers *(jongleresses)* who, together with twenty-nine men musicians' *(ménestrels)* combined in Paris in 1321 in order to establish for themselves statutes, which were sanctioned on the fourteenth of September of that year." In New York, the musicians' Union started admitting women to membership only in 1903, although it had been in existence for many years.

* * *

A major Symphony Orchestra now, the Indianapolis Symphony, includes ten women in its personnel this season. Nine of these instrumentalists are employed in the violin, viola and cello sections of the organization. The tenth is the harpist. Like the rest of their colleagues, the ten women are engaged for a period of 21 weeks and are on weekly salaries. Mr. Fabien Sevitzky is the Conductor and Mr. Franklin Miner the Manager of the ensemble.

* * *

"Thank you very much for all the interesting data...It was, to say the least, illuminating and somewhat disconcerting to find out how much we didn't know about how and where women found and can find their place in music," says a letter to *Women in Music*. The letter comes from Sylvia Canick, Program Chairman of K M E, a Hunter College Music Sorority.

* * *

More than ten years ago, a distinguished Baltimorean foretold "a future that will universally recognize a Lanier Day as a national school event. For, few names in American literature have equalled in ever widening popularity among the literati and the critics of this country and abroad as that of Sidney Lanier," who, incidentally, urged in 1880 that women cultivate orchestral instruments.

* * *

Speaking of Lanier, the poet-musician, the concert with which the Orchestrette Classique will pay a special tribute to his memory on Monday evening, January 10, at the Carnegie Chamber Hall, will feature a flutist, Ruth Freeman, as the assisting artist in a Mozart Concerto. It will also introduce Beatrice Merlau, clarinetist, who will render solo parts in a Prokofieff piece on the program. The program starts at 8:30 and will be under the direction of Frederique Petrides.

ORCHESTRA IN SOUTH FOUNDED BY WOMAN

Knoxville, Tenn.—This community's participation in the steadily increasing activities of women in the symphonic field is crystallized through the work of Mrs. Bertha Walburn Clark, who is the founder-conductor of the new Knoxville Symphony Orchestra, an ensemble of some fifty players from both sexes.

The origin of Mrs. Clark's venture dates back to that time, quite a few years ago, when she was playing professionally the violin for one of the local hotels. One evening a flutist brought his instrument along and started "music making" with her and her accompanist. The management welcomed the innovation, the flutist was soon imitated by other enthusiasts for ensemble-playing and it was thus that Mrs. Clark acquired a nucleus of players around which she has gradually built her active and ambitious non-professional orchestra.

Composed only of local talent throughout its groping days, the Knoxville Symphony has had a considerable increase in ranks in the last two years or so, i. e., sometime after the Tennessee Valley Authority established its headquarters in Knoxville, the nearest city to Norris Dam. Away from home and family, a number of instrument players in the TVA project turned to music for recreation and joined the orchestra. Some of these, sceptical at first as to the wisdom or the advisability of playing under feminine leadership, have long ago been converted, so to speak, and are now as pleased with their affiliation as the rest of the players, men and women, who have for years known and appreciated Mrs. Clark's qualities as musician and leader.

The Orchestra was recently given a measure of financial help from local business men. Its goal is to become eventually a community project, supported by every Knoxvillite.

Erno Rapee will be the next guest-conductor this season of the Woman's Symphony of Chicago.

Orchestras of women represent "one of the most important musical movements in recent years," according to Mr. George Schaun, music critic of the *Baltimore Sun*. (In America, this "movement" took its first serious step back in 1888 when Caroline Nichols founded the Fadettes Orchestra in Boston.)

Published by the "Orchestrette Classique", 190 East End Ave., New York City.

Hiring a female brass player was certainly not common during this period since brass and percussion players probably faced the most blatant discrimination. Ammer (p. 206) states that **Leona May Smith,**

> . . . foremost woman trumpeter of this period, was featured as a soloist at Radio City Music Hall and worked both with Fred Waring's Pennsylvanians and the Goldman Band, two of the nation's leading popular ensembles. Yes, she said in 1938, there "is" a future for women musicians, but they must somehow overcome the common critic's attitude: "This is a commendable performance, considering the player is a woman." The best steady income for a woman musician, Smith concluded, was teaching. Though Smith played first trumpet with the National Orchestral Association, performed with the Chautauqua Symphony, and won a number of awards, she devoted most of her time in succeeding years to teaching brass instruments to high school students (Clipping Files, NYPL).

Nadia Juliette Boulanger was an organist, conductor, music critic, lecturer, and composer who came from a family of musicians. At the age of twenty-one she won the Second Grand Prix de Rome for her cantata *La Sirene* in 1908. According to Ammer (pp. 134–36),

> One of the most important influences on American composers . . . was a French teacher of composition, Nadia Boulanger (1887–1979). Trained at the Paris Conservatory, where Gabriel Fauré was among her teachers, she began to teach privately when she was only seventeen (in 1904) and five years later joined the Conservatory faculty. In 1913 her best-loved pupil, her younger sister Lili, became the first woman to win the First Grand Prix de Rome for her cantata *Faust et Hélène,* and Nadia decided to devote herself entirely to teaching and give up composition, for which she believed she had little talent compared to her sister's. Her sister died of tuberculosis five years later, and after Lili's death Nadia's pupils became, in effect, her family. . . . Her principal influence over American composers was exerted at a summer school of music founded at Fontainebleau (near Paris) in 1921, the American Conservatory (whose director she became in 1949). . . . In 1936 and 1937 she conducted the Royal Philharmonic Orchestra of London in Gabriel Fauré's Requiem, the first woman conductor they ever had. She also was the first woman to conduct the Boston Symphony, the Philadelphia Orchestra, and the New York Philharmonic.

At the outbreak of World War II, Nadia came to the United States and taught for several years at Wellesley College, Radcliffe College, and the Juilliard School of Music.

| News, Facts, Activities | # WOMEN IN MUSIC | Orchestras; Conductors |

Vol. III No. 6   *Edited by Frederique Petrides*   February, 1938

Three Southern women are known to have conducted symphony or opera orchestras so far. The first of these was Emma Steiner. Born in Baltimore, Md. in 1867, Miss Steiner who died in New York in 1929, conducted over 6000 performances of light and grand opera. The second Southern woman conductor is Bertha Walburn Clark, whose Knoxville Symphony Orchestra gives another concert next month. The other is Elizabeth Woodson. She led, not so very long ago, the Virginia Symphony Orchestra, a W P A project.

* * *

Has Father Malachy, that gentle and lovable character of the stage, recently passed another miracle? According to an *Associated Press* story, four sisters and their mother, all of them members of a girls' jazz orchestra in Texas, gave up their orchestra work last month and joined a religious order.

* * *

The only WPA project of its kind, the Commonwealth Women's Orchestra of Boston, plays often in various communities in Massachussetts. Its latest concert was scheduled for the tenth of February in Belmont, Mass.

* * *

The discussion of professional problems confronting **women in** orchestras, constitutes the **principal** aim of a new column in the *Metronome*. The column was introduced last month and is conducted by Leona May Smith, the wellknown cornetist.

* * *

Musical Vienna was divided a few years ago into two debating camps on the question of whether women should or should not lead orchestras. The cause of that controversy was Carmen Studer-Weingartner, wife of the celebrated conductor. Shortly before the outbreak of the Sino-Japanese War, Mme. Weingartner conducted in Tokio as assistant to her husband. Soviet Russia was the next country in line for concert work by the couple. This, however, ill-pleased the Nazi Music Associations, which have now placed Weingartner on their blacklist, according to a German publication as quoted by the Music Section of the *New York Times*. As added result of this blacklisting, no performance will be given of a new version of " Carmen " arranged by Mme. Weingartner and which was to be presented by the Munich Opera House.

Mlle. Nadia Boulanger

Mlle. Nadia Boulanger, the internationally known French musician, who came to America this month in order to conduct, as guest, the Boston Symphony Orchestra on Feb. 18 and 19, and also for a semester's teaching at Wellesley and Radcliffe, is no stranger to New York, Boston and the other American cities which she visited on her previous two trips in 1925 and 1937.

Landing in New York for the first time on December 31, 1924, as the guest of Mr. and Mrs. Walter Damrosch, Miss Boulanger appeared as organ soloist with the New York Symphony, Walter Damrosch conducting, on Jan. 11, 1925, in Aeolian Hall. Her offerings at that performance included a composition by Lili Boulanger, her exceptionally gifted but short-lived sister; also, the work of one of her many American pupils in composition, Aaron Copland's "Symphony for organ and orchestra", a work dedicated to her. These compositions she also played twice in Feb., 1925 with the Boston Symphony, Serge Koussevitzky conducting.

A few days following her American debut as organ soloist, she gave her first lecture-recital in America at the David Mannes School in this city. She spoke then on the life of Gabriel Fauré, one of her teachers, and was presented to the audience by Mrs. David Mannes, who decribed her as a *superwoman, one whose mentality, knowledge of music and sincerity are rarely found in one person.*

Around that time, a writer for *Musical America* asked Miss Boulanger "whether as an outsider she could hear any traits in the so-called American music which were not European." Growing enthusiastic, she answered: "There is a distinctly American personality in your music, and there are some very fine artists. It is Europe's duty to assist the Americans by stressing the fact that our older culture is just a starting point for them..."

For the first time in history, Harvard students will study at Radcliffe this semester—in order to sit in Miss Boulanger's classes.

Her guest-conducting of the London Philharmonic Orchestra last November, and her work with the Boston Symphony this month will be remembered as two historically important "firsts" in the activities of women and orchestras.

Helen Kotas, first horn player of the Woman's Orchestra of Chicago, earned a fine compliment for herself and her organization, when she was asked, last month, to play a week's performances with Frederick Stock's celebrated Chicago Symphony, as one of the eight horns required for Strauss' "Ein Heldenleben." Incidentally, the Woman's Symphony of Chicago closed another successful winter season early this month.

* * *

Before she started her famous column in behalf of lonely hearts, broken hearts, yearning hearts etc., Beatrice Fairfax, the Emily Post of love, served on the staff of the old *New York Herald*, having been lured there "by the idea of doing music criticism and attending all the best concerts," says Ishbel Ross in her unique book, *"Ladies of the Press."*

* * *

An oversight in these columns last October was recently corrected by *Women in Music*, through information supplied by it for an item in *Newsweek*. According to this information, Emma Steiner, Ethel Leginska and Antonia Brico have also conducted, as guests, in America's major symphonic field.

* * *

Unless no publicity man had anything to do with it, the story of the scatter-brained member of a girls' orchestra in New York, who forgot her tuba, of all things, in a taxi, represents *some* case of absentmindedness, indeed!

* * *

It wouldn't be a bit surprising, should some playful but uninformed observer happen to remark one of these days that it is beginning to look as though if there is any Vivaldi to be played this season by women's groups in New York, the piece must be for four soloists, or, else...no Vivaldi on the program. Last month, the N. Y. Women's Symphony played Bach's transcription for four harpsichords of the Concerto written originally by Vivaldi for four violins. The same work, in its original form this time, will be rendered by the Orchestrette Classique, Frederique Petrides conducting, on Monday evening, March 7, at the Carnegie Chamber Music Hall. Hinda Barnett, concertmaster of the Orchestrette, Anne Littman, Ilene Skolnik and Frieda Reisberg will be the soloists in this beautiful composition by Vivaldi.

Published by the "Orchestrette Classique", 190 East End Ave., New York City.

Among her approximately six hundred American composition students were George Gershwin, Aaron Copland, Walter Piston, Roy Harris, Roger Sessions, Louise Talma, Virgil Thomson, David Diamond, and Elliot Carter.

Petrides kept two pieces of autographed correspondence from Boulanger. One (not dated) was an apology for not having written sooner and included hopes of meeting in April when she was to return. This was written on stationery with letterhead from the Cunard White Star *RMS Queen Mary.* Another, March 18, 1939, from Gerrys Landing, Cambridge, Massachusetts expressed appreciation for Petrides's many kindnesses.

Walter Damrosch (1862–1950) conductor, composer, and music educator was the son of Leopold Damrosch (1832–85), violinist and conductor. Among his other activities, Walter Damrosch presented a *Music Appreciation Hour* for school children (1928–42), which was carried on NBC and heard throughout the United States and Canada.

Leona May Smith. Courtesy Music Division, The New York Public Library.

Nadia Boulanger, lecturing at Radcliffe, 1938.

VOL. III, NO. 7, APRIL 1938

In a letter dated July 10, 1937, **Gertrude Herliczka** wrote that the **Vienna Women's Symphony** had been in existence for sixteen years and had always been conducted by Professor Julius Lehnert, who also had conducted the Vienna Opera. It seemed that the orchestra personnel thought he was "too old" to continue, but he had supported them so well over the years they could not "send him away."

Petrides included **Lonny Epstein's** biographical sketch in her program notes for the January 30, 1939, concert.

> Lonny Epstein, Faculty Member of the Institute of Musical Art (Juilliard), was born in Germany and has given many concerts in this country and abroad. Years ago, she played as soloist with the Friends of Music in New York City under the direction of Arthur Bodanzky. Her European activities include performances as soloist with such distinguished conductors as Otto Klemperer, Fritz Steinbach and Fritz Busch. This is Miss Epstein's second appearance, as guest-soloist, with the Orchestrette.

Epstein was born in 1885, joined the Juilliard piano faculty in 1927 and became an American citizen in 1938. In 1964 she retired from teaching and moved to Switzerland. She returned in March of 1965 and at eighty performed an all Mozart program at Juilliard and the Newark Museum. She had scheduled several other appearances but on March 9, 1965, died of a heart attack. Several students wrote of her influence in the March 1965 *Juilliard Newsletter*. Michael Bassin remembered "her vast knowledge of the life and music of Mozart, her performances on her reproduction of Mozart's own piano, her wonderful musicianship . . . her warm personality."

Carl Friedberg (1872–1955) had studied with Clara Schumann and was teaching at Juilliard at the time this article appeared. *Baker's Biographical Dictionary of Musicians* lists his better-known pupils as Percy Grainger, Ethel Leginska, and Elly Ney, but there is no mention of Lonny Epstein or Julia Smith (see *Women in Music,* March 1939). In fact, Epstein studied with him from 1902 to 1906 at the Cologne Conservatory. Friedberg attended Petrides's concerts and wrote to her as "an admiring colleague."

Grace Kleinhenn Thompson Edmister was born in Ohio on August 2, 1890. As a young girl she studied with local teachers, began teaching piano at fifteen, and received her bachelor's degree in 1908 from Defiance

| News, Facts, Activities | # WOMEN IN MUSIC | Orchestras; Conductors |

Vol. III No. 7   *Edited by Frederique Petrides*   April, 1938

Shortly before Hitler annexed Austria, Gertrude Herliczka, the Viennese-American conductor, who is at present leading symphonic concerts in Italy, drew the attention of *Women in Music* to the existence of the Vienna Women's Symphony Orchestra. This organization was founded in 1921 by Julius Lehnert, who has conducted it ever since. At the beginning, due to the lack of available women players of the wind instruments, the orchestra had limited its repertory to string selections only, rather than include men players in its ranks. This short-sighted policy has long ago been abandoned, however, and besides its regular concerts, the orchestra gave also in recent years a number of radio performances. Naturally, now that the swastika is flying over Vienna, it remains to be seen whether this feminine enterprise will or whether it will not be permitted to function.

* * *

About four years ago, Lonny Epstein, the noted pianist and assistant of Carl Friedberg, offered to donate her services as soloist with the Orchestrette Classique, provided the group would live to show a measure of permanence in its activities. Early this year, Miss Epstein was reminded of her pledge. Accordingly, she will be the assisting artist at the concert with which the Orchestrette Classique will conclude its fifth season on Monday evening, May 2, in the Carnegie Chamber Hall. She will render on that occasion Mozart's Concerto in E flat Major. (Koechel 271.)

* * *

The fashion report which is reprinted here in part pertains to the world's oldest Woman's Symphony in existence and is borrowed from a recent issue of the *Pacific Coast Musician:* "The Woman's Symphony Orchestra of Los Angeles is about to transform itself into a 'tone color vision' at its next concert... The idea, we understand, originated with Concertmistress Bessie Fuhrer Erb, of having the members of the orchestra dress in outer garments whose hues would harmonize (theoretically vibrate sympathetically) with the tone quality of their instruments. Now, whether this splendiferous visual display will be of contemplative classic agreement or be modernistically clashing remains to be seen. It is rumored that the orchestra's membership, all women, will eye the audience with curiosity in an effort to get the latter's reaction." (This group is one of the three women's orchestras in California.)

According to the Woman's Page of the *N. Y. Sun,* when a Boston reporter asked Nadia Boulanger how it felt being the first woman to ever conduct the Boston Symphony, she answered. "I've been a woman for a little over fifty years, and have gotten over my initial astonishment. As for conducting an orchestra, that's a job. I don't think sex plays much part."

* * *

Transradio Press Service announced the news that Grace Thompson of Albuquerque, N. M., will direct the Albuquerque Symphony next month at the New Mexico Folk Festival,— a week-long celebration which will "include folk dancing, drama and songs, together with native Indian music." Mrs. Thompson is head of the music department of the University of New Mexico and was to lead, on March 6, the Albuquerque Civic Orchestra of which she is the conductor, reported *Musical America* in February.

* * *

A musical journalist in London is known to have publicly confessed his aversion, not so very long ago, to the sight of any man conducting a women's orchestra. Fortunately, this funny aversion is not shared by intelligent persons. In America, six women's symphonic groups are led by men. Hyman Schandler is one of them. His Cleveland Women's Symphony Orchestra, composed of some 85 players, was scheduled to give another concert on the sixth of April.

* * *

Women instrumentalists of Chicago have an organization of their own, says the *Musical Leader*. The Society's aim is to create professional opportunities for its members.

* * *

For days following its first full-scheduled Town Hall apearance early last month, New York music lovers were talking in high praise of the seven-year-old Durieux Chamber Ensemble: nine women string players excellently rehearsed by Mr. Durieux, their conductor.

* * *

Mme. Marie Flagstad, mother of Kirsten Flagstad, the Metropolitan Opera soprano, is known as the "musical mamma of Norway" and "has conducted several operas,'" according to the *New York Times*. Recently, she served as assistant conductor for eight performances of *Carmen* given by a mixed professional and amateur company in her native land.

The following comments, written around the American debut of the Vienna Ladies' Orchestra, were published in the September 30, 1871, issue of the *Woodhul and Claflin's Weekly* (New York), and are reprinted as a reminder to all young musicians: "The Vienna Ladies' Orchestra, has acquired confidence since their first debut and give pleasure to their audiences by their easy and graceful playing. Their first performance created a disappointment. Not that they did not do well, but because they did not realize the extravagant praise with which they had been heralded. The free advertising of living wonders is a business necessity, but the excessive adulation carries its own reaction. The public are surfeited with these to come and to be reports. No one believes in managerial puffs and the end is a comparison between promise and performance which is almost always to the disadvantage of the artist."

* * *

An item in Ethel Peyser's book, *The House that Music Built*, shows that as early as 1898 Carnegie Hall heard a concert given within its famed walls by the the New York Women's String Orchestra. The second women's unit which has been heard in that auditorium was Leginska's American Woman's Symphony in 1932. However, the only ensemble of its kind with three Carnegie Hall seasons to its credit so far, is Antonia Brico's four-year-old Symphony Orchestra. Incidentally, this group concludes its current offerings with a concert on April 26th.

* * *

Stories on woman's work, past and present, in the orchestral field, find increasingly their way into the pages of American publications. A recent addition is the survey of women's orchestras which appears in the *Woman's Almanac* for 1938. Based on data originally compiled and presented by *Women in Music* up to April, 1937, this survey ends with the very appropriate remarks that no longer a novelty, women's orchestras must strive for musical excellence if they wish to survive. Besides the press, however, radio executives are also beginning to appreciate the subject of women in orchestras. Thus, Station WJZ of the NBC's Blue Network and also *Transradio Press Service* of Station WOR presented Frederique Petrides, conductor of the Orchestrette Classique, in two background talks last month on this hereto little known activity of women musicians ever since the seventeenth century.

Published by the "Orchestrette Classique", 190 East End Ave., New York City.

College. In 1912 Kleinhenn married Lewis Thompson, a choir director and cellist. In 1918 she was stricken with tuberculosis, and she and her husband moved to New Mexico in an attempt to save her life. She recovered and began teaching piano and theory at the University of New Mexico, where she founded its department of public school music. With the backing of the Albuquerque Rotary Club and a colleague, flutist William Kunkel, she also founded a community orchestra. She was appointed conductor and Kunkel the assistant conductor. The goal was to make good music available for everyone, and the local business community helped underwrite the cost. The charge for a concert ticket was twenty-five cents, and they gave their first concert on November 30, 1932; they played to an audience of two thousand.

In 1941 Kleinhenn appeared as piano soloist with the orchestra. By then her marriage to Thompson had ended, and she married William R. Edmister, a businessman from Columbus, Ohio, where they resided until his death a number of years later. In 1970 she returned to Albuquerque to give help and support to the Albuquerque Symphony and in 1972 was invited to guest conduct a concert (Ammer, 213–15).

Kirsten Flagstad had in fact begun her education and career by study-ing with her mother, Marie, who was a coach at the Oslo Opera.

SIDNEY LANIER MEMORIAL CONCERT

MONDAY EVENING
JANUARY 10, 1938
AT 8:30

CARNEGIE CHAMBER
MUSIC HALL
154 W. 57th ST., N.Y.C.

ORCHESTRETTE CLASSIQUE

FOUNDED IN 1933

FREDERIQUE PETRIDES
Conductor

Soloist: Ruth Freeman, *Flute*

P R O G R A M M M E

Ouverture "Die Heimkehr aus der Fremde"	Felix Mendelssohn
Suite No. 1 in C Major	Joh. Seb. Bach
Concerto for the Flute in D Major	Wolfgang A. Mozart
Pastorale d'été	Arthur Honegger
Ouverture on Yiddish Themes	Serge Prokofieff
Symphonie IV (Italian)	Felix Mendelssohn

Orchestra	$1.25 (Tax Free)
Balcony	75c (Tax Free)

Kindly make checks payable and send to the Orchestrette Classique. 190 East End Avenue, New York City. For phone orders, call BUtterfield 8-0835.

| News, Facts, Activities | WOMEN IN MUSIC | Orchestras; Conductors |

Vol. III No. 8   *Edited by Frederique Petrides*   June 1, 1938

The Affirmative Side

It is to be hoped that the Committee for Recognition of Women in the Musical Profession will prove instrumental in stirring up talk on the mixed orchestra. As far as research reveals, relatively few men musicians and critics have ever cared to commit themselves in print, one way or another, on this controversial subject. At the same time, these findings of *Women in Music* show that the men who have publicly expressed themselves, unconditionally or otherwise, in favor of women for orchestras, outnumber those who have taken an opposite stand. Some of the representative opinions, friendly to the cause of the mixed orchestra, are reprinted in this issue as added encouragement to women players and their apologists.

* * *

LEOPOLD STOKOWSKI in 1916: "....An incomprehensible blunder is being made in our exclusion of women from symphony orchestras. The particular spirit that women put into music, their kind of enthusiasm, their devotion to anything they undertake would be invaluable in the formation of symphony orchestras. .... In addition to their delight in their work, they are quick to get the meaning of a score, nimble-witted in taking in a new idea and most conscientious about appointments, time and practice....When I think of women as I see them in the musical world, what they are capable of doing, their fine spirit, excellent technique, I realize what a splendid power we are letting go to waste in this country and in other countries too..."

* * *

HANS KINDLER in 1935: "I am all for women in orchestras."

* * *

SIDNEY LANIER in 1880: "With the exception of the double bass and the heavier brass,—indeed I am not sure that these exceptions are necessary—there is no instrument in the orchestra which a woman cannot play successfully...Let our young ladies ...address themselves to the violin, the flute, the oboe, the harp, the clarinet, the bassoon, the kettledrum. It is more than possible that upon some of these instruments the superior daintiness of the female tissue might finally make the woman a more successful player than the man...Besides, the qualifications required are more often found in women than in men; for these qualifications are patience, fervor, and fidelity, combined with deftness of hand and intuitiveness of soul."

A New Organization

A significant group activity of New York women instrumentalists was launched on Wednesday, May 18th, when something like one hundred and fifty feminine players, all of whom are members of the Musicians' Union, Local 802, attended a meeting in Steinway Hall. The meeting was called by the two-month old Committee for Recognition of Women in the Musical Profession, an organization which proclaims as a right the granting of full employment opportunities for women instrumentalists.

Through interested women's clubs and consumers' societies, the Committee plans to exert pressure on the New York Philharmonic, the Metropolitan Opera, the National Broadcasting Company and other organizations in New York City which do not employ women musicians except harpists. Its most immediate consideration, however, is to induce through protests, radio sponsors selling women's products to start including feminine instrumentalists in their orchestras. Should this method prove fruitless, a boycott will be undertaken.

Various women's organizations have promised their support for the success of the group, which was formed after a report to the Musicians' Union (18,000 men and 800 feminine members) showed that women hold only ninety-five steady jobs in New York orchestras.

Speakers at the meeting were: Jean Schneider, director of the Committee and one of its founders; Miss Antonia Brico of the New York Women's Symphony; Mary Dreier of the Women's Trade Union League; Felicia Laurie of the Consumers' League; Mrs. Isabel Walker Soule of the League of Women Shoppers. Also, Joyce Barthelson, chairman of the Committee; Ruth Wilson, the organization's publicity director, and Catherine Newton, its financial secretary.

MUSICAL AMERICA (Editorial) in 1935: "...The time has come when orchestral players of the gentler sex must be seriously considered....Our conductors will find in the ranks of women players fine artists, who will co-operate with male members if given the opportunity. Artistically, we believe that orchestras made up of members of both sexes may in the future reveal tonal qualities as yet unknown and unsuspected. In a supposedly forward-looking world, the hitherto closed doors of symphony orchestras should be opened to 'make way for the ladies.' "

The Affirmative Side

SERGE KOUSSEVITZKY: "Time was when Henry Wood was the only first flight conductor who not only preferred, but insisted on including women in his band. Now we have another conductor of world-wide reputation, Koussevitzky, going out of his way to expatiate on the beneficial effects of the feminine element in an orchestra. (I wonder if the Russian knew he was quoting Mozart when he spoke of the greater 'appreciativeness and responsiveness' of women as regards the conductor's intentions?) A special point Koussevitzky insisted on has often been stressed by Henry Wood, that their presence conduces to good discipline." — Dame Ethel Smyth in 1933.

* * *

H. T. FINCK in 1902: "Possibly there will be a division of labor, the violins and woodwinds being assigned to women, the basses and percussion instruments to men."

* * *

FREDERICK HUBER (Baltimore's Municipal Director) in 1937: "The five women whom we engaged for the Baltimore Symphony have unquestionably proven satisfactory, in terms of ability, dependability and attendance. As a matter of fact, there was never any doubt in my mind about this. They are very fine musicians and I am 100% for them."

* * *

WM. J. HENDERSON in 1935: "There is no good reason why women should not be employed in orchestras. The chief question to be asked is whether they can play as well as men. After that, other considerations may be taken up. Can a conductor force discipline among the women as well as he can among the men...? Can women endure the severe strain of long and repeated rehearsals? That as well as other questions become individual rather than general. All a conductor needs to know is not whether women can fill all the requirements, but whether the particular women can, whom he contemplated engaging..." ——(in 1932) "Why should we not have women conductors and orchestras?..."

"A chair and stand in the ranks, or even the conductor's desk and baton of the symphony orchestra offer great and growing opportunities for women," reads the comment with which *THE ETUDE* announces for its July number an article on "Women in Orchestras" by Frederique Petrides, conductor of the Orchestrette Classique.

Published by the "Orchestrette Classique", 190 East End Ave., New York City.

| News, Facts, Activities | WOMEN IN MUSIC | Orchestras; Conductors |

Vol. IV No. 1 *Edited by Frederique Petrides* July, 1938

The San Francisco Symphony Orchestra was the first major group in America to admit women to its playing personnel, according to Ronald F. Eyer in *Musical America*. Former conductor Alfred Hertz "began the practice by engaging a woman violinist. He ended by having eight women in the string sections, and most of them are still there."

* * *

"Life is a circle," comments Ethel Leginska, who now commutes from London, her home, to Paris for the bi-monthly classes she holds in composition and conducting. "I began as a pianist, became a composer, then a teacher, and then a conductor. Now I am completing the circle."

* * *

How tradition punished another gifted girl musician was recently explained by Mr. Samuel Chotzinoff in the *New York Post:* " I happen to have first-hand knowledge of the kind of thing that talented girl musicians frequently come up against," he wrote. "Auditions were held not long ago to recruit players for one of the best American orchestras, and a young lady horn player presented herself as a candidate. Civility demanded that the lady be heard, though it was a foregone conclusion that she could not possibly make the grade. Well, sir, she played her horn superbly and the judges were so impressed that they went into a huddle to see whether anything could be done about her. Here was a girl who could blow the "Siegfried" horn call in tune and without " breaking. " Time and again the distracted jury summoned her into the room and put her through the most difficult horn passages in the symphonic repertoire and each time she passed the test with flying colors. But tradition being what it is she never got the job. . ."

* * *

Pittsburgh's own woman conductor is Miss Gwen Treasure. Her all-feminine String Sinfonietta is often heard in concert and in local radio broadcasts.

* * *

A little more "night music" was heard on the evening of June 10th in New York City, when the "Penthouse Little Symphony Orchestra" held its first concert at the residence of Mrs. Schuyler Schieffelin. The group is composed of 23 players from both sexes and "was founded by Miss Mary Schieffelin during the season of 1936-37 to provide opportunity for instrumental enthusiasts to play in friendly ensemble." Frederique Petrides is the conductor.

Mme. Carreno's Pluck

How a revolution forced her to lead an Opera Company for a while is the little known story that was told, many years ago, by the late Teresa Carreño, who still is remembered as one of the greatest piano virtuosos.

According to this story, her cousin, Guzman Blanco, while serving as President of Venezuela, commissioned her to import to that Republic an Opera Company which would be subsidized by the Government. She accepted and the following season went to Venezuela in the capacity of an "impressario." It so happened, however, that her company landed in Carácas, the capital, just as a revolution had broken out in the interior. And, no sooner had her artists landed when the pro-revolution element in that city thought up a plan to break up the opera in order to discredit the régime with the people.

During rehearsal one morning, as Mme. Carreño walked across the stage, a bottle dropped from the flies and broke at her feet. This was the beginning of the hostilities and there followed several attempts to break up the opera performances which were given under strong police protection. Then rumors spread that the opera house was to be blown up—a ruse in order to keep the public from attending.

The company's one and only conductor, who, incidentally, had been imported from Spain, was the next target. He was bombarded with threatening letters ordering him to take the next boat to Spain, if he valued his life. Frightened out of his wits, the maestro took to his bed and stayed there, refusing to return to his post. Now, such a development compelled the "impressario" to put the concertmaster on the podium; but, a prima donna threw a chair at him during a rehearsal and he resigned. Mme. Carreño then asked her first cellist to lead. He was so bad, however, that when the curtain fell after the first act, her business manager begged Mme. Carreño to do the conducting herself. He insisted that she could certainly do better than the cellist, and, at last, won, finally, her promise that she would direct the orchestra from that moment on.

Mme. Carreño's pluck, as emergency leader, created a very favorable impression and the pro-revolutionists saw that they would only lose ground by annoying a woman. So, they let the company work in peace and prosperity for the rest of the season, under her conductorship.

Miriam, the sister of Moses, was very musical and may well be regarded as one of the first leaders of women singers of her race. After the Israelites had crossed the Red Sea, she "took a timbrel is her hand, and all the women went out after her, with timbrels and with dances. And Miriam answered them: Sing ye, sing ye to the Lord, for He had triumphed gloriously, the horse and his rider hath He thrown into the sea." (Ex. XV. 20-21).

* * *

With this number, *"Women in Music"* enters its fourth year. Ever since it was started, this "miniature journal" has been considerably encouraged by seeing many of its contents reprinted in various publications, daily and periodical, in and outside of New York City.

* * *

The reason why women players are not employed by radio stations was described, some few weeks ago, in Chicago's *Musical Leader* by Mrs. Florence French, its editor-publisher. She wrote: "With few exceptions, the gentlemen who conduct the great orchestras of the country have never yet been able to employ women musicians. They do not openly discriminate. They simply take care there shall be no vacancies. The radio stations *actively and openly discriminate against women* orchestral players. Women are absolutely boycotted by the powers that be. Although many women are superior to some of the men playing in some of the orchestras, it is useless for a woman to make application for a place in an orchestra. It behooves the radio stations to give women a place in their "sustaining" programs.. That radio stations should so drastically discriminate against woman orchestral players is incomprehensible..."

* * *

Although women orchestras are of European origin, nevertheless, there are more of them in present day America than in the Old World.

* * *

The Schumann Club in Bangor, Maine, sponsors a Ladies' String Orchestra, which functions under the direction of Anna Torrens Dymond.

* * *

Chicago has no less than four women conductors. Gladys Welge, of the Woman's Symphony of Chicago, is one of these musical directors. The others are, Ebba Sundstrom who leads her Symphonietta; Lillian Poenisch, conductor of the Chicago Woman's Band;and Fanny Arnston-Hassler, conductor of the Women's Concert Ensemble.

Published by the "Orchestrette Classique", 190 East End Ave., New York City.

VOL. IV, NO. 2, SEPTEMBER 1938

This information concerning **Ruth Kemper** came from a letter Caroline B. Nichols wrote to Petrides in 1937 about Kemper and her activities. Kemper had been a member of the Fadettes. In 1930 Kemper was on the faculty of the Salzburg Conservatory, and in 1931 she conducted a concert in Vienna.

Howard Barlow (1892–1972) was associated with CBS as a conductor 1927–32 and as general music director, 1932–43. He directed the NBC radio series "The Voice of Firestone" from 1943 to 1961.

| News, Facts, Activities | # WOMEN IN MUSIC | Orchestras; Conductors |

Vol IV. No. 2   *Edited by Frederique Petrides*   September, 1938

So far as available records show, only six women are known to have conducted in America's symphony or string orchestra fields between 1890 and 1924; however, at least twenty more have led similar groups in this country between 1924 and 1938.

* * *

A feud between Parisian men and women musicians was reported a few weeks ago by Transradio Press in one of its daily *Women Make the News* broadcasts over WOR. According to this source, the discord is "all due to the fact that women's orchestras are now so popular (in the French Capital) that some of the men musicians are having a tough time getting work in night clubs and cafes.

"The feud reached such a height recently that 16 police guards had to be called out to quell a riot. They found a young woman violinist holding a crowd of men, and using her violin case as a weapon of defense.

"The violinist, Estelle Francen, had just arrived at an assembly hall in Montmartre where hopeful musicians gather for bookings. A group of men musicians spied her and an angry shout rang out: 'There is one of them.'

"The men looked so threatening that Miss Francen turned and ran. They pursued her until she sought refuge in a subway entrance. For 20 minutes, she kept the men musicians back as she slashed vigorously with her violin case. The 16 gendarmes arrived just in time to save the girl musician from the angry mob of jobless men musicians."

* * *

A special concert of chamber music, featuring unusual combinations of string and wind instruments in a program of interesting music, will be rendered by various players of the Orchestrette Classique during the season of 1938-39 under the auspices of their organization. This concert will be given in addition to the regular orchestral series of the ensemble.

* * *

Ruth Kemper, who led last year the Boston Women's Orchestra (WPA), directed again on August 17th,—this time the Greenwich Symphony Orchestra, a unit of the Federal Music Project in New York City.

* * *

The distinction of being the first organization of its kind in any University is claimed by the Women's Band of the University of Wisconsin, 43 players.

Mothers' Band

A most elementary group, to be sure, and yet the Mothers' Rhythm Band in the down town section of New York's East Side is so delightful in its attitude toward music-making that *Women in Music* takes pleasure in bringing it to the attention of its readers.

Twelve mothers, ranging in years from thirty to sixty, are in this Band, which meets at the Stuyvesant House every Tuesday. These housewives pride themselves on being always on time and on never missing a rehearsal, except under the most dire emergency. Woe to any woman who is so unprofessional a musician as to plead "a headache" or that "Johnnie has a toothache." If she cannot arrange her home affairs so that she can give two hours a week for music-making,—well, it is too bad for her; she just has no place in the Stuyvesant House Band.

Writing about the Mothers' Band in *The Etude,* Sarah Simkins quoted as follows some of its members: "I play in a band and now I am a person," says Mama Abramowitz, as she relaxes after a rehearsal. "I wash the dishes and clean the house and teach the children to be nice. I go to their plays and watch them shine. But now I play in a band myself and I am a person."

"We play high class pieces same as my Izzy plays," explains Mrs. Markowitz, adding proudly: "Our band plays Schubert's *Rosamunde* and Bach's *Musette.*"

"We play the new songs too—the ones our children hear at the movies and on the radio," chimes in Mrs. Cohen enthusiastically, "like *Old Lady* and *Pennies from Heaven.*"

The mothers themselves requested the formation of this group, which happens to be one of three similar units taught by WPA music teachers. While at rehearsal, they play on their cymbals, tambourines and drums, rendering among other pieces, such things as Sousa's military marches and the Strauss waltzes; and, quite often, they request songs they sang in their childhood.

A mother-participant told Katinka Stollberg, the Federal Music Project teacher who guides the band: "It makes me feel that life is not yet over for me," and she added in Yiddish: "I thought my brains had dried up—but now I know that I can still learn new things."

Antonia Brico's appearance as guest-conductor at the Lewisohn Stadium on the 25th of July represents the first instance of a woman wielding the baton at a concert of the New York Philharmonic - Symphony Society.

* * *

God must have forgotten to pay much, or any, attention to the Frenchman's prayer. But, the letter Monsieur de Warville wrote from Boston in 1825 and in the course of which he had appealed, so to speak, to the Almighty to guard Boston womanhood against "the malady of perfection" as pianists, that epistle is still remembered if only once in a very great while. It was recently quoted as follows by Mr. Leonard Liebling's *Variations* in the *Musical Courier:* The "city has young women here and there who are shyly beginning to practice the piano-forte in primitive manner, but the charming novices are so gentle, so complaisant, and so modest, that the proud perfection of art gives no pleasure equal to what they afford. God grant that the Bostonian women may never, like those of France, acquire the malady of perfection in this art! It is never attained but at the expense of the domestic virtues."

* * *

Milwaukee's own woman conductor is Pearl Brice, leader of the MacDowell Club Orchestra in that city.

* * *

An orchestral work, which received its first performance through the women's orchestra that played it in April, 1937, was heard again, a few weeks ago, in the course of the radio concert with which Howard Barlow and the Columbia Broadcasting System began in New York City their Sunday afternoon performance of unpublished works by talented American composers. This work is Julia Smith's *Episodic Suite,* which, written originally for the piano, was arranged for orchestra at the recommendation of Frederique Petrides. The women's ensemble that gave it its introductory hearing last year is the Orchestrette Classique. Incidentally, the Orchestrette, of which Miss Smith is the pianist since 1933, will play another work of hers before the end of the coming season.

* * *

Sixteen women's orchestras, if not more, are expected to give concerts in the course of a new season. The total number of players in these sixteen groups in America is about 900.

Published by the "Orchestrette Classique", 190 East End Ave., New York City.

VOL. IV, NO. 3, OCTOBER 1938

Pauline Juler (1914–?) was born in London and made her debut in 1932 with Sir Malcolm Sargent conducting. She played first clarinet in the the New London Orchestra and performed concertos with the London Symphony Orchestra. Her work was "regularly broadcast to further confirm her position as a leading exponent of her instrument in Great Britain" (Palmer, 264).

News, Facts, Activities		Orchestras; Conductors

WOMEN IN MUSIC

Vol. IV. No. 3 · *Edited by Frederique Petrides* · October, 1938

The astrologist who predicted increasing activities for feminine musicians in 1938 was right after all. A glance at that phase of activities which pertain to women orchestral players shows that quite a few of them were employed by newly-started ensembles since last January. And recently, the orchestra of the New Friends of Music, New York, has engaged the following players for this, its first, season: Frances Blaisdell, first flute; Lois Wann, first oboe; Ellen Stone, first horn; Mara Sebriansky, first violin section; Lotta Hammerschlag, viola.

* * *

What if Mayor LaGuardia can boast of having wielded the baton over a symphony orchestra? What if his Honor is not without laurels as music commentator? Can he point out to a captain in his police force who has led a woman's symphony during his régime? No. And here is where the Little Flower is overshadowed by the record of the late John Hylan, whose police captain, Paul Henneberg, directed a sixty-piece Woman's Symphony in 1925. Incidentally, that orchestra was organized by Beatrice Oliver, oboist, and had played in various public parks under the auspices of Mayor Hylan's Music Committee.

* * *

Before resuming its regular activities, the Orchestrette Classique will present fourteen of its players in a special program of rarely heard chamber music on Monday evening, November 14th, in Carnegie Chamber Hall. The program, as arranged by Frederique Petrides, will also feature the guitar virtuoso, Julio Oyanguren, in a Schubert quartet and a number of solos as well. Lonny Epstein, the pianist, will be soloist at the concert with which this miniature symphony of 28 women will start in January, 1939, its sixth season's orchestral series.

* * *

NBC's Conductor, Frank Black, says: "I have no feeling against women being used in any orchestra that I conduct."

* * *

One wishes that there would be other feminine organizations, besides the Mu Phi Epsilon national sorority, to contribute annually towards the maintenance of women's orchestras. The ensemble to which this sorority lends a measure of financial support is the ever-busy Woman's Symphony of Chicago, now in its fourteenth season.

Opinions

Do some orchestral instruments look unesthetic only when played by women? Mr. Samuel Chotzinoff, music critic of the *New York Post,* does not think so. He wrote in his column: "The very idea of a lady horn player was held, not so long ago, to be simply killing. It was presumed that the mere sight of a lady manipulating the slide of a trombone could not be borne soberly." . . . Yet, "of all the instruments in an orchestra it may be said that the violin and the harp only are ornamental. The rest are merely contrivances for sound, and they look unesthetic no matter what sex plays on them."

* * *

The molesting of an employed French woman violinist by a resentful crowd of Parisian male musicians this past summer brought forth the following editorial comment in the September 15th issue of *Musical Courier:* "This is a large country with plenty of room for feminine activity in music and the gentler sex need not fear the opposition meted out in France by male musicians to their performing sisters . . . "

* * *

Roberta Trent of Indianapolis should feel very encouraged. Her directing of a non-professional string sinfonietta at the recent convention of Sigma Alpha Iota in Milwaukee impelled the editor of *Musical Leader* to call her "an extraordinarily clever conductor," who "should become one of the leading women conductors."

* * *

How do young American men musicians feel toward the mixed orchestra? It is to be hoped that many of them share the sentiments expressed to us in the following letter from Mr. Sigurd Bockman, member of the Minneapolis Symphony Orchestra. He says: "Perhaps the fact that I'm quite young has something to do with it, but I believe women participating in an orchestra do add a valuable spirit, a certain quality which the majority of men fail to capture, though they may appreciate it. I don't think, either, that a touch of refinement that they bring would be entirely amiss. I was somewhat startled to realize the scope of women's activities as you have them presented and I don't have a doubt in the world that they will gain in leaps and bounds."

A woman orchestral performer played an important part in the musical education of Ferde Grofé, the American composer, arranger and conductor. The woman? None else but his mother, who "was a very fine musician indeed," according to Mr. Grofé. Back in 1888, Mrs. Grofé played in a "ladies orchestra" at Feltmann's Open Air Garden in Coney Island. It was she who taught her now famous son to read and write music even before he knew his abc's. Moreover, besides drilling him on the piano and violin, she also assisted him to write a "Mozartean" opera in his boyhood days.

* * *

"Forty-five men and a girl," — such should have appropriately been, up to the end of last month, the parenthetic designation of Albany's Knickerbocker Symphony Orchestra. And this was due to the participation of Helen Enser, New York player of the French horn, in the summer and September concerts of this unit of the Federal Music Project. Proclaiming the hornist as "the best" he ever heard, Ole Windingstad, conductor of the ensemble, made further use of her ability. He featured her as soloist on Sept. 12th, in Mozart's Concerto in E. flat major.

* * *

An English clarinet soloist, Pauline Juler, who at present is in this country, informs us that women players are still employed by such an important orchestra in London as that of the British Broadcasting Company; also, that the oboe desks in the London Symphony Orchestra are occupied by Evelyn Rothwell, first, and Natalie Caine, second desk. (Ed. Note:- One of the earliest instances of a woman oboist with a professional orchestra in London dates back to the 1880's. She worked for the Carl Rosa Opera Company. As for violinists, the Moody-Manners Opera Company, formed in London in 1897, employed a number of them.)

* * *

Among the first women in Czarist Russia to play in the San Petersburg Symphony was Elfrieda Bos Mesteschkin. For years now an American by adoption, this artist is widely respected in New York's musical circles. Besides her other affiliations, she serves, as concertmaster, the N. Y. Women's Symphony, now in its fifth season.

Published by the "Orchestrette Classique", 190 East End Ave., New York City.

News, Facts, Activities

WOMEN IN MUSIC

Orchestras; Conductors

Vol. IV. No. 4   *Edited by Frederique Petrides*   December, 1938

Nadia Boulanger of Paris will appear as guest-conductor with two major American orchestras this season. One of these organizations is the New York Philharmonic-Symphony, the direction of which she will share with Mr. Barbirolli in a special concert, under the auspices of the Philharmonic-Symphony League, on February 11. The other orchestra is the Detroit Symphony. Miss Boulanger will lead one of its concerts in the course of this season, according to published reports.

* * *

An unconventional angle was injected into the subject of women for orchestras by *Musical Leader* through the following paragraph in its issue of October 22:—"*Women in Music,* a clever brochure . . . , carries much information concerning the 'weaker sex' in music. Quoted from the *Musical Leader* is an article concerning discrimination against women orchestral players by leading conductors who cannot throw tradition to the winds. But there is something more than tradition that prevents major orchestras from employing women. Lady patrons of symphony concerts are in the large majority. They go to symphony concerts to see an orchestra of men. There would be a big slump in attendance if the orchestra became a mixed affair. A woman's symphony orchestra is a specific organization. A man's orchestra should be manned by men, because this is the only way it can be maintained."

* * *

Lonny Epstein will appear as soloist with the Orchestrette Classique, Frederique Petrides, conductor, on January 30. She will render Mozart's *G. Major concerto* for Piano.

* * *

Some of the best instrumentalists in New York's concert field are employed by Edgar Carver's newly started all-girl band, 20 musicians. This unit plays popular music and was heard for two weeks last month at a World's Fair exhibit.

* * *

Back in 1908, Philadelphia was the first American city to see a stage production that included a "ladies' orchestra" and a woman orchestral leader in its plot. The occasion was the American premire of "A Waltz Dream," the famous Viennese operetta which presented this novelty. Incidentally, the girls' orchestra-in-the cast idea has been used rather increasingly by Hollywood in the last two or three years.

Case History

Many years prior to his death in 1924, John C. Freund, the founder and editor of *Musical America,* told in his magazine the following story:

"Many years ago, at a time when even a woman pianist was almost unknown here, and a woman violinist would have been almost hooted in the streets if she carried her violin case, I became acquainted with a little Russian or Polish Jewess, who had extraordinary musical talent. Her parents were, as most of her class are, extremely poor. A German musician of great talent, but also himself poor, recognized the child's ability and gave her lessons for nothing for years.

" She tried to get engagements without success; and finally she went to the conductor of a well-known orchestra and applied for a position. He heard her play and said: 'My dear young lady, you have so much ability and talent that you would put to shame some members of my orchestra. I could use you as my first violin, but if I were to put you in that position there would be not only a riot on the stage, but one in the audience.'

"For a time, her parents having died, the young girl endeavored to maintain herself playing around in little restaurants on the East Side, till the usual love tragedy happened with an unscrupulous Italian singer. She had a child which, from lack of proper nourishment, died.

"In her despair, she took to drink and sank and sank—till she sank out of sight.

"Here was a genius, a great talent, who was told that she had no show, no opportunity because she was a woman . . . "

*

In the course of a newspaper interview which the great Marian Anderson gave months ago to Mr. William J. King, music editor of the *New York Sun,* she said: "There is a spiritual called *Stay in the Field.* I think the title might be a motto for Negro musicians. If they will stay in the field, they will be recognized according to their worth." Although the Aframerican contralto's' remarks were uttered expressly for artists of her own race, nevertheless, they should also have a direct inspirational appeal to talented women players and conductors.

The New York City Federation of Women's Clubs is perhaps the first powerful feminine organization in New York, if not in America, to take an official stand in favor of the mixed orchestra. At its recently held convention in New York City's Hotel Astor, this organization, acting upon the recommendation of Mrs. Otto Hahn, Chairman of its department of Fine Arts, endorsed "the principle of equal opportunity for qualified women musicians" in opera, theatre and radio orchestras.

* * *

Her love for music cost Mrs. William Brown Meloney, editor of the widely syndicated *This Week,* her job as reporter on a Washington paper many years ago, says Ishbel Ross in *Ladies of the Press.* As Marie Mattingy, Mrs. Meloney was assigned to meet a Senator in the Congressional Library, but she became so absorbed in a collection of rare music that she forgot her appointment, and when she came out of her stupor, she couldn't find him. Her editor fired her: "If you love music that much," he told her, "you will never make a good reporter."

* * *

Margaret Horn of Pittsburgh is scheduled to lead this month a public concert of the String Ensemble (fifty one strings and woodwinds) of her home town's Tuesday Musical Club.

* * *

A girl student-player contributes this disarming admission in *Up Beat:* "Our Band is playing mighty well "We're feeling prouder and prouder, "And if somebody slips a bit, "We just play all the louder."

* * *

Girl baton twirlers have become quite a vogue in 1938, a vogue which, it is said, some old male band leaders are beginning to find rather difficult to compete with. One hundred of these drum majorettes led bands at this year's American Legion Convention in Los Angeles, and "completely stole the show." Girl drum-majoring has been going on for about six years in America.

* * *

Julia Smith, pianist of the Orchestrette Classique since 1933, is one of those talented and methodically proceeding young American composers who invariably succeed in having their work performed in public. Thus, one of her earlier compositions, the *Little American Suite,* which was premiered in 1936 by the Orchestrette, will be played again this season, this time by the Oklahoma Symphony Orchestra.

Published by the "Orchestrette Classique", 190 East End Ave., New York City.

| News, Facts, Activities | # WOMEN IN MUSIC | Orchestras; Conductors |

Vol. IV No. 5   *Edited by Frederique Petrides*   January, 1939

The skill and musicianship with which Gertrude Herliczka, the Viennese-American conductor, directed a concert of the Paris Symphony Orchestra on Dec. 4th, "class her among the leading conductors of the day", according to the Paris correspondent of *Musical Courier*.

• • •

Women in Music regrets exceedingly its error last month regarding one of Mlle. Nadia Boulanger's forthcoming American engagements as guest conductor . The distinguished French musician will not lead a concert of the Detroit Symphony, as previously reported here, but is to direct the last half of the program which the six-year-old Dayton Philharmonic presents on January 23 in Dayton, Ohio.

❊ ❊ ❊

A musically trained reporter, Miss May Garrettson Evans has founded the Preparatory Department of the Peabody Conservatory of Music in Baltimore, Md. While working for the *Baltimore Sun* in the early part of the nineties, she was commanded by her editor to dig up stories. She complied by writing a piece on her pet idea for a Preparatory Department in the Conservatory. The story was featured prominently by her paper and some time later Miss Evans outlined to the Conservatory a detailed plan on her idea. However, as those in charge of the Institution did nothing with her suggestion, she and her sister opened in 1894 a school of their own. The experiment proved a huge success and in 1899 their school was merged with the Conservatory as its Preparatory Department. Miss Evans headed it until 1929.

• • •

Jessica Marcelli led, not so long ago, the Berkeley (Cal.) Community Orchestra in "a well-planned concert",

• • •

Long before the mixed orchestra received its present-day impetus in various parts of the country, Conductor Albert Stoessel was regarded by his students up at the Juilliard as favoring the inclusion of women in symphonies. That this student opinion was and is . well grounded was proven once more at last month's Carnegie Hall concert of the Oratorio Society of New York. Mr. Stoessel's orchestra for this performance had again included a number of women instrumentalists. (Hinda Barnett, Lois Wann and Ruth Freeman, members of the Orchestrette, were among those who played in this concert.)

Union Candidate

Ever since 1900, the year when the New York Musicians' Union (Local 802) started admitting women into membership and up to very recent days, the average female member "did not care to take advantage of her privilege to vote" at union elections. She paid her dues and assessments, but stayed away from headquarters because women "should feel very much out of place among the men." An injudicious attitude, of course, but that was that.

As a contrast to the past, the elections held by Local 802 last month showed that New York women musicians are becoming more and more conscious of their union rights and responsibilities. For, a good many of the 850 female members showed up to vote. In addition, one of them was included among the candidates for a place in the Local's Executive Board. Incidentally, the latter did not win, but hers is anyway the distinction of being the first woman candidate in the history of the country's biggest and most powerful musical union.

The woman candidate was Elizabeth Barry, a trombone player. She was endorsed by both parties which ran in opposition to President Rosenberg's victorious ticket and received around 2700 votes out of the more than 9000 votes which were cast.

• • •

The recently-formed Brico Symphony, successor to the disbanded New York Women's Orchestra, is scheduled to make its Carnegie Hall debut on Monday evening, Jan. 25th. Antonia Brico is the conductor of this new mixed ensemble of 80 players.

• • •

Under the playful caption "Weaker Sex Weakened", the New Year Issue of the *Billboard* carried this item on what has happened in recent days of stress and strife to the "Eleven Debutantes", a non-union all-girl dance orchestra: "Kansas City, Mo., Dec. 24.—Police clubs rapped on heads, women pulled each other's hair and consternation in general reigned the other night outside the ultra Kansas City Club when an 11-piece orchestra attempted to run a picket line to play for a dance in the swank club's ball-room, where a strike was in progress. The non-union band failed to enter. . . and the 'Eleven Debutantes' vowed they would stay on non-union locations in the future, declaring that the pickets were tough "on gowns, coiffures, horns and equipment'."

Madame Yolanda Mero, the Executive Director of the Musicians' Emergency Fund, had, in years gone by, the secret ambition to conduct an orchestra. As, however, she believed at that time that "a woman in front of an orchestra looks ridiculous as a rule," she let that ambition of hers go unsatisfied.

• • •

Winifred Christie, this month's soloist with the Woman's Symphony of Chicago, recently met a violinist in London whose deviation from the pitch was such that it seemed as if she were tone deaf. A or E it made no difference to her. Learning that Miss Christie was the English pianist, the violinist volunteered the information that she formerly studied the piano, but gave it up in favor of the violin, as she considered the piano far too easy for her mentality!

* * *

The subject of women for orchestras attracted more journalistic handling in 1938 than at any other previous time. With the exception of one belligerent voice, all opinion was in favor of the mixed orchestra. As for the dissenting stand, this was taken in the August number of Pittsburgh's *Musical Forecast* by one of its columnists, Dr. Gaylor Yost who believes that "women have no place in any symphony orchestra except one composed entirely of women" and that "a technically competent male instrumentalist is still more desirable than any equally competent female instrumentalist. . . "

* * *

Dr. Howard Hanson, as quoted in the *Musical Leader:* "For many years I have felt that a woman in the orchestral field should compete with men on an absolutely even basis. I should without hesitation prefer a woman to a man if she proved to be the better performer and musician."

* * *

The works of two young American composers, Ulric Cole's *Two Sketches for String Orchestra* and Gian-Carlo Menotti's *Pastorale* will be included in the program which the Orchestrette Classique, Frederique Petrides, conductor, presents on Monday evening, January 30th, at the Carnegie Chamber Music Hall. Featured artist for this concert will be Lonny Epstein, the admirable pianist, who will render Mozart's *G. Major Concerto*. The other billed compositions are: Gossec's *Symphony in E flat Major* and Haydn's *Clock Symphony*. The latter work will be played in grateful memory of Henriette Weber, the New York music critic, who died in Minneapolis on August 2, 1938.

Published by the "Orchestrette Classique", 190 East End Ave., New York City.

VOL. IV, NO. 6, MARCH 1939

Petrides wrote her own program notes, and the following information appeared in the March 21, 1939, Orchestrette Classique program.

> Asger Hamerik was born in Copenhagen on April 8, 1843. He was the son of a church historian and showed early talent for composition. He inherited a definite religious atmosphere at home, hence the religious character of many of his compositions. His teachers were Gade, von Bulow and Berlioz.
>
> Hamerik had already become known in Europe as a composer when he was called in 1871 to Baltimore as Director of the Peabody Conservatory of Music, a position which he held for 26 years. In 1900, he made a tour of certain European cities giving concerts of his orchestra works, after which he settled in his native country, the King of which had bestowed the Knighthood upon him in 1890. He died in Copenhagen on July 13, 1923.
>
> His "Symphonie Spirituelle" is one of his many orchestral works. It was composed in 1896 on occasion of his 25th anniversary as Director of the Peabody Conservatory and was played, probably for the first time, on Tuesday, May 5, 1896, in an all-Hamerik program given at that famous institution.

| News, Facts, Activities | WOMEN IN MUSIC | Orchestras; Conductors |

Vol. IV No. 6   *Edited by Frederique Petrides*   March, 1939

A week before the evening of Saturday, February 11, when Nadia Boulanger, — *The First Lady of the Music World* — conducted a concert of the New York Philharmonic Symphony Orchestra, given in her honor under the auspices of the Philharmonic Symphony League, Mr. William G. King, devoted his column *Music and Musicians* in the New York *Sun* to an interview with the distinguished French artist.

"She was the first woman to conduct the Royal Philharmonic Society of London, the first woman to conduct the Boston Symphony, and she will be the first of her sex to conduct the Philharmonic-Symphony Orchestra of New York in a winter-season concert," observed Mr. King. . . . Her record of 'first times for a female,' however, does not interest her, and she is a little regretful that it interests anybody else. God made her a woman, she says, but he also made her a musician, and of the two facts, the second is of much greater importance . . . "

* * *

Despite the prejudice existing in various quarters against women as conductors, Miss Boulanger has conducted thus far some of the world's most important orchestras, including the Paris Philharmonic. What then was the reaction of players in these symphonies towards her as conductor? And how does she think musicians in general react to a woman's baton?

"In Paris and elsewhere there has always been a fine camaraderie between myself and the musicians," she told Mr. Louis Biancolli of the New York *World-Telegram*, a few days prior to her New York appearance, as guest-conductor. "A priori, a man has more authority over a body of men. If men were perfectly frank they would say they prefer to be led by a man. They have never made me feel that, however...'

* * *

New Yorkers had not as yet had the opportunity of judging her as conductor when Brailsford Felder advanced in *Cue* the following opinions:

"The prejudice against women conductors, which lurks in the bosom of every orchestra player, breaks down instantly when it comes in contact with Mlle. Boulanger's master touch. For she is one woman who knows her business. She can read a score as readily as the best of men conductors, and her vast knowledge and understanding of music has the virile intellectuality usually achieved by men . . . "

Nadia Boulanger

In profound admiration for the genius of Nadia Boulanger, *Women in Music* departs in this issue from its customary news policy and devotes most of its space to a summary of opinions expressed last month by New York newspaper music critics on her work as conductor as well as to some of her own views on the same subject.

The handful of persons who, like the editor of *Women in Music*, had the good fortune to attend the only full rehearsal Miss Boulanger had with the Philharmonic, saw her start to work in an unostentatious but positive and matter-of-fact way. That rehearsal, which lasted over two hours, she conducted with superb self-confidence, mastery and warmth. The feeling of genuine camaraderie between conductor and player was there and one could see and feel at once that the gentlemen of the orchestra were enjoying their musical tasks under her inspiring command.

It was eight hours following that rehearsal when she made her appearance, as guest, with the Philharmonic-Symphony of New York, an appearance which electrified and enthused everyone present.

* * *

The large, brilliant and knowing audience which heard the long-anticipated Boulanger concert in Carnegie Hall, "proved by its applause that it was finding the realization no less thrilling than the anticipation," to quote from the review in the New York *Post* by Mr. Edward O'Gorman.

New Talent

Julia Smith, whose opera, "*Cynthia Parker*" was given its premiere last month in Denton, Texas, has written a "*Concerto for Piano*," which will be introduced this month in New York by the Juilliard Orchestra at the Juilliard School Auditorium. Since 1933, this talented composer has been the pianist of the Orchestrette Classique, which commissioned her to write her two earlier works: the "*Little American Suite*," and the "*Episodic Suite*," both played for the first time by the Orchestrette under the direction of Frederique Petrides.

Miss Smith is a fellowship student at the Juilliard, where she studied the piano under Mr. Carl Friedberg, but specializes in composition under Mr. Frederic Jacobi.

Through the courtesy of the Peabody Conservatory of Music in Baltimore, Md., the Orchestrette Classique, in the program for its concert on Tuesday evening, March 21, will include the "*Symphonie Spirituelle*" by the late Asger Hamerik, who was the Director of that Institution for more than twenty years.

Miss Boulanger performed her various parts in the elaborate and unusual program for that evening, "with brisk, composed, unfaltering self-confidence, with sure efficiency and ease, wasting no time, assuming no poses; completely certain of herself, engrossed in the task before her. She paid only the briefest attention to the ardent applause of the astonished and admiring audience, smiling faintly as she bowed, and she left the stage as soon as she could when the work of the moment was accomplished . . . '" Thus, Mr. Lawrence Gilman in the New York *Herald-Tribune,* who also devoted to the visiting artist a two-column dithyrambic essay, under the heading *First Lady of the Music World,* on February 5.

* * *

(The latter part of the program at this concert was conducted by Mr. John Barbirolli, while Miss Boulanger played the organ in a composition by her short-lived sister, and took one of the piano parts in Mozart's E flat *Concerto*).

* * *

The New York *Times,* through Mr. Noel Strauss, opined in part: "...In whatever capacity she exhibited her talents this amazing artist moved with a like authority, profound understanding and skill . . . She was completely the master of style in all she touched, and her insight into the character and needs of the highly contrasted works she set forth was unfailingly deep and penetrating..."

* * *

"Miss Boulanger, in a long, loose white dress, was as free from manner and as much at ease as if Carnegie Hall were her home and audience and performers her family," said another critic, Mr. Pitts Sanborn in the New York *World-Telegram*, adding: "Conducting (without a baton and also without a trace of self-consciousness), she disclosed signal ability as a leader, whether the composition were instrumental or vocal, and she brought fluence and authority to her piano playing . . . "

* * *

Remarking that "her platform deportment was a model of self-effacement for conductors everywhere," Mr. Oscar Thompson, wrote in the New York *Sun* that " . . Miss Boulanger played her several roles easily and with unmistakable authority... on this memorable . . . evening of music . . . "

* * *

Miss Boulanger will be the guest-conductor for two concerts of the Philadelphia Symphony this month.

Published by the "Orchestrette Classique", 190 East End Ave., New York City.

Concerning **Alicia Hund's** conducting, it was recorded that, "to the horror of the men in the orchestra and audience, Alicia conducted a performance of her own symphony" (Cohen, xxx).

It is ironic that pianist, educator, lecturer, and writer **Amy Fay** (1844–1928) did not think **Alicia Hund's** conducting "a very becoming position," since otherwise Fay's life and career reflected modern feminist theories. Born in Mississippi, her first teacher was her mother, Charlotte Emily Fay. She was twelve when her mother died, and she moved to Boston to live with her sister and her brother-in-law. There, she studied at the New England Conservatory and in New York but at the age of twenty-five went to Europe alone and remained there for six years. She eventually studied with Franz Liszt and wrote about him in her book *Music Study in Germany* (1880), which remains an important historical source on Liszt and a student's life abroad during this period. She was also published in other journals. She dedicated herself to her career and determined that she would never marry (or even do housework). "The questions Amy Fay addressed; namely, how to secure a position that brings personal satisfaction, how to tap into emotional support systems, and how to find meaning and purpose in life in a world disproportionately organized and managed by men, are questions women address today" (McCarthy, abstract).

Hetty Turnbull asked Petrides for about sixty *Women in Music* copies, which she planned to distribute at monthly meetings of the Women's Musicians Association in Boston. Turnbull wrote September 3, 1937, that she knew many women who were no longer employed as musicians but would appreciate news of those who were.

Albert Stoessel (1894–1943) was an American violinist, composer, and conductor.

French composer, poet, singer, and pianist **Louise Angelique Bertin** (1805–77) composed several operas as well as other works. Her father was the editor of the *Journal des Debats,* which allowed her entry in the musical world and enabled her to enlist the support of Berlioz who was attached to that paper as a critic.

In 1937 Petrides had commissioned **Paul Creston** (1906–85), an American composer, to write a marimba concerto. Nearly forty years later on October 20, 1975, he wrote a long, fond letter to "Ricky." He

| News, Facts, Activities | # WOMEN IN MUSIC | Orchestras; Conductors |

Vol. IV No. 7   *Edited by Frederique Petrides*   April 15, 1939

A new light opera based on the early history of New Mexico—libretto by Helen Bagg, music by Nino Marcelli — will be produced next month by the College of Fine Arts of the University of New Mexico in Albuquerque, under the direction of Mrs. Grace Thompson, head of that University's music department. Last spring, Mrs. Thompson, who conducts the Albuquerque Symphony as well, directed at the New Mexico Folk Festival—a week-long celebration which included folk dancing, drama and songs, together with native Indian music.

* * *

Formed in November 1937, as a result of the "success of similar organizations in New York, Chicago and Philadelphia", the St. Louis Women's Symphony Orchestra, 60 players, gave its first concert, a few weeks ago, under the direction of Edith Gordon, its organizer.

* * *

Mr. Deems Taylor believes that women cannot play the tuba. And that's that! !

* * *

Described by its editor as a Women's Edition, the current issue of Pittsburgh's *Musical Forecast* presents a very informative survey of feminine contribution, past and present, to Music and the Arts by women in Pittsburgh, Pa. A specially featured notice which appears in this number of the *Forecast* speaks of *Women in Music* as being "an interesting monthly account of facts and news concerning women in music throughout the world".

* * *

Greece's only major symphony orchestra, the one which Dimitri Mitropoulos led in the past as its regular conductor, includes a number of women players in its violin section.

* * *

Two women have promised to conduct their respective orchestras at the annual Convention of the National Federation of Music Clubs which is held in Baltimore Md., next month, and which will last six days. One of these musicians is Sarah Yott, organizer and director of the Junior Civic Symphony (40 players) in Albuquerque, N. M. The other is Miss Margaret Horne, who will lead the all-feminine ensemble (52 players) of Pittsburgh's Tuesday Musical Club. Incidentally, Miss Horne and her ensemble played over Station WEAF on April 8. They participated in a program which featured as speaker, Mrs. Vincent Hilles Ober, the President of the Nat'l Federation of Music Clubs.

Developments in Germany

Back in the eighteen seventies, a famous American pupil of Liszt, the late Amy Fay, saw Alicia Hund conduct a Symphony Orchestra in Berlin in a composition of her own, whereupon she wrote, as follows, in a letter which she included later in her widely circulated book *"Music Study in Germany"*: "All the men were highly disgusted because she was allowed to conduct the orchestra herself. I did not think myself that it was a very becoming position, though I had no prejudice against it. Somehow, a woman doesn't look so well with a baton directing a body of men."

Recently, however, another woman conducted an orchestra in Berlin, whereupon Geraldine de Courcy wrote as follows in *Musical America:* " Mary Ann Culmer of Indianapolis... made her first appearance as an orchestral conductor at a concert with the Berlin Landes Orchester . . . Her readings .... won her a veritable triumph, which was warmly seconded by the members of the orchestra who were apparently as fascinated by her able achievements as the public."

"The ovation tendered Miss Culmer, " continued the *Musical America* correspondent, "was especially noteworthy in view of the fact that Germans have always had a deep-seated prejudice against women in the orchestra. With the exception of the occasional employment of women harpists in theatre orchestras, they are strictly excluded from orchestral organizations in Germany. It was therefore interesting to note from a speech made recently by Dr. Peter Raabe, President of the Reichs Music Chamber, that owing to the scarcity of young talent in the ranks, the hitherto unwritten law against the employment of women players will be relaxed in the future".

* * *

A Boston horn player, Hetty K. Turnbull reports the formation of the Women's Symphony Orchestra of Boston. Stanley Hassel, faculty member of the New England Conservatory of Music, is the conductor of this new aggregation of 66 players.

* * *

Chicago's *Musical Leader*, one of the best friends *Women in Music* has had practically since its inception in 1935, quoted, editorially, in one of its recent issues, the comment originally made here about Conductor Albert Stoessel's friendly attitude towards the mixed orchestra. The quotation was prefaced with words to the effect that *Women in Music* is "an excellent little brochure, one that is informative and entertaining...."

Victor Hugo wrote the libretto of *Esmeralda*, a five-act opera which was set to music by Mlle. Louise-Angelique Bertin and was presented for the first time in Paris in 1836, enjoying very few performances. Based on one of his novels, the opera was received by an antagonistic class of Parisians as a work the music of which was as artless as its libretto. Years later, the French writer remembered his collaboratrice with *La Sagesse*, a poem he dedicated to her and with which he closed the last volume of his fugitive verses *Les Rayons et Les Ombres*.

* * *

When Louis Biancolli, of the New York *World-Telegram*, remarked to Nadia Boulanger that in some quarters it was regarded as undignified for a woman to play the double bass or kettledrums in a symphony orchestra, she replied: "Women do many things in life which are more harmful to their dignity than playing kettledrums."

* * *

Although scheduled originally for April 24, the season's final concert of the Orchestrette Classique will be given instead on Monday evening, May 1, at the Carnegie Chamber Hall. Hinda Barnett, concertmaster of the ensemble, Lois Wann, oboist, Beatrice Merlau, clarinetist, and Ruth Freeman, flautist, are the soloists. Included in the program for this occasion are two American works, Samuel Barber's *Adagio* for Strings and Paul Creston's *Partita* for flute, violin and strings. Frederique Petrides is the conductor of this group of 28 players.

* * *

" Many are the problems confronting girl musicians in the popular music field," according to a letter which comes to us from Mr. Paul Denis, one of *Billboard's* editors in New York. His interesting and illuminating letter reads in part as follows: "Girl dance band musicians must not smile at patrons, because they, the girls, may be misunderstood. They must not engage in friendly banter with male patrons near the bandstand because the women patrons may suspect that the girl musicians are trying to steal their men. The girl musicians must be dressed attractively but not flashily — so that they will impress as musicians and not as flirts. The leader of the girl band must be careful, too. She must be genial, and more attractive than the rest of the orchestra — but she, too, must be careful not to appear to be flirting with male patrons. '

"Because of this situation, many high class hotels are afraid to book girl dance bands . . . "

remembered that Petrides had paid him fifty dollars for the work and that it had become so popular that he had made a band arrangement of the orchestra part. He referred to the Concerto as her "brain-child" and remarked that every time he received a royalty check from Schirmer, he raised his eyes to heaven and murmured, "God Bless Ricky."

St. Louis
Women's Symphony Orchestra

EDITH GORDON, Conductor

FIRST SYMPHONY CONCERT

Monday February 27, 1939

Soldan High School Auditorium 8:30 P. M.

Admission Fifty Cents

St. Louis Women's symphony, during a rehearsal. St. Louis Post-Dispatch, *June 19, 1938.*

VOL. V, NO. 1, NOVEMBER 1939

David Diamond (b.1915) wrote Petrides on July 9, 1939, asking her to consider programming one of his works. He was twenty-four and had just returned from France and a Guggenheim Fellowship. He wrote that one work, an *Elegy in Memory of Maurice Ravel,* needed a string orchestra, tympani, tenor drum, and glockenspiel and that it was a work he particularly had in mind for her and the Orchestrette. She agreed and scheduled the work for their November concert—the first performance of the work with his new instrumentation. Before the concert he wrote in detail of how the work should be performed and the specific changes he wanted made in the manuscript. In 1940 Petrides commissioned a work, Concerto for Chamber Orchestra, from Diamond.

| News, Facts, Activities | # WOMEN IN MUSIC | Orchestras; Conductors |

Vol. V. No. 1   *Edited by Frederique Petrides*   November, 1939.

The First Battle of Our Century:

—The members of the Women's String Orchestra — an organization started in New York in 1896—waited one, two, three years for the critics to go and cover *en masse* their concerts, which were given either at the Steinway Hall, the Waldorf or at the Mendelssohn Hall. They went on waiting, hoping, but all in vain.

Then dawned 1900—the year which found the Women's String Orchestra in a challenging mood. Its members had gotten tired of waiting for the critics. Accordingly they retaliated by inserting in their fall announcements the following challenge: "That a few critics have ignored the concerts of the Society given to audiences of 900 people, while their papers chronicle any parlor musicale, however insignificant, seems to show that there is still a pressure of prejudice against serious artistic work by women in any new line."

Shortly before the Women's Orchestra rose in protest, Camilla Urso, the famous violinist of those days, wrote to Mr. Carl V. Lachmund, the group's conductor: ". . . in the face of untold obstacles, you have conquered and no one rejoices over it more than I do — knowing the prejudices existing against women as orchestral players."

The challenge to the critics was not taken seriously. The String Orchestra enjoyed three more well-patronized seasons. Finally it disbanded, leaving the field to the other active orchestras of women in this country.

Throughout its existence, the Orchestra played music written only for string ensembles. It was started with 18 players who, by 1900, had been increased to thirty-eight. That its work was good is attested by the fact that among those to bestow critical praise on it were Henry T. Finck of *New York Evening Post* fame and also Mr. William J. Henderson, who, at that time was with the *N. Y. Times.*

It Was a Very Hard Test for Chivalry:

"The Boston Symphony Orchestra is in danger of serious dissension and all because women have invaded the musical field. The Symphony players are nearly all Germans, and when not playing at Symphony Hall are mostly engaged in giving instructions", said a story which appeared in the "New York Herald" of April 19, 1902, and which is reprinted here in full.

"Many of their pupils are young women, about twenty of the latter at the present time being members of the Fadette Women's Orchestra.

This organization did not attract much attention in Boston until a few weeks ago when it appeared at Keith's theatre and made a decided hit.

"In fact, it drew such audiences that the management decided to engage it for a few weeks during the summer season. This meant that the Symphony players were to be supplanted by women, the Symphony players having been for several years a summer attraction at Keith's

"Now the players who had no part in teaching the women are blaming the men who made them so proficient that they have been able to get the "snap" musical engagement of the summer, while the Symphony players are making their contracts with summer hotels."

The Women's Orchestra discussed in the preceding lines, was started by Caroline B. Nichols, a Boston violinist who said in 1910: "I don't believe in rules. The minute you make them the girls try to find a way to get around them and that makes them sneaky."

Miss Nichol's group was active up to the end of the World War.

Hinda Barnett, the Orchestrette's concertmaster, will also play this season in the Orchestra of the New Friends of Music.

Orchestras in music-minded ancient Egypt often numbered 600 instruments and included about 12,000 persons in their supporting choruses. Not only did women also play in these orchestras, but they gradually superseded the male artists in them.

Looking Backward

For five years now we have been listening, talking, reading and scurrying around — in order to gather facts, anecdotes and news about women in the orchestral field, past and present.

Each issue added another gray hair to our head, but the gray hair turned back to normal when the issue came off the press and we had the genuine pleasure of feeling certain that quite a few people would enjoy our material.

Five years is a long time and we already feel mellow enough to lean back and enjoy a Remember-When mood as we go over our earlier issues. And, because we feel that some of our readers might like to share our Remember-When mood we are reprinting in this number three of the representative research stories from our first volume.

A Wartime Story and its Aftermath:

Sir Henry Wood, the prominent English conductor, saw no earthly reason why he should dismiss the women players whom he had admitted in the ranks of his Queen's Hall Symphony during the World War.

What if those artists were not men? He had found them to be hard-working, capable and reliable musicians. Their presence in the orchestra had improved the tonal qualities of its strings. Furthermore, the men played the better for competition.

True, the War was over and his women players had been hired in emergency days. But with peace restored, and the Tommies back from the battlefields, the London musical marts were full of idle men musicians. And, since something had to be done to reduce unemployment, the majority in the profession felt and insisted that Sir Wood should fill all his choirs with men musicians.

But, Sir Wood was not in the least willing to yield. He had always held that sex discrimination has no place in music and the arts. What if the majority of his fellow-conductors and musicians in England, did not agree with him on this subject? He was not going to sacrifice his principles for the sake of precedent. Accordingly, he stood determinedly by his female instrumentalists—a stand which infuriated the opposition. So much so, indeed, that by 1924, all English musical unions were closed to women.

Faced with such developments, women musicians in London retaliated by forming not only a musical union of their own, but the British Women's Symphony Orchestra as well under Miss Gwynne Kimpton. The Orchestra, a co-operative enterprise, was under the immediate patronage of the Queen. It made its debut in the spring of 1924 and has been commendably active ever since.

An Elegy in Memory of Maurice Ravel,

written by David Diamond, the young American composer, is included in the program with which the Orchestrette Classique, Frederique Petrides, conductor, begins its seventh season on Monday evening, November 6, at the Carnegie Chamber Hall. The soloist for this concert will be Lonny Epstein, who will play Mozart's Concerto in C Minor (K491). Incidentally, this will be Miss Epstein's third appearance, as soloist, with the seven year-old Orchestrette.

Published by the "Orchestrette Classique", 190 East End Ave., New York City.

Izler Solomon (1910–87) was born in St. Paul, Minnnesota, and he remained in this country during his career. He conducted a number of major orchestras, as well as being music director of the Brandeis Festival in Waltham, Massachusetts, and the Aspen Music Festival. He was dedicated to programming twentieth-century American music.

Violinist, conductor, and teacher **Ruth Haroldson** (1909–82) was born in Brookings, South Dakota. She earned a bachelor of music degree at the American Conservatory of Music, where she was a pupil of Leo Sowerby and Jacques Gordon. She also studied under Mischa Mischakoff, former concert master for Toscanini in the NBC Symphony, and with Sascha Jacobson of the Los Angeles Philharmonic. In 1933 Haroldson accepted a position as professor of violin at Whittier College in Whittier, California, and remained at that institution until her retirement in 1965.

During her first year at Whittier College, she founded and conducted the Whittier Symphony. This was a women's group that eventually became the Whittier College Community Orchestra. In 1957 the name of the orchestra was changed to the Whittier Symphony when it gained financial assistance from Los Angeles County and the city of Whittier. In 1964 the name was again changed, to the Rio Hondo Symphony. In 1939 she also began conducting the Women's Symphony of Los Angeles. In 1953 Haroldson founded a Youth Symphony, which she conducted for five seasons.

Haroldson owned and performed on a Stradivarius violin made in 1717.

"A Tribute to Miss Ruth Haroldson," program from an appreciation dinner, May 8, 1965, Whittier College.

Finnish conductor, teacher, and composer **Heidi Sundblad-Halme** (1903–73) studied piano and composition at the Sibelius Academy and in Berlin. In 1938 she founded the Helsinki Women's Orchestra and continued as its conductor until 1968. She wrote for orchestra, piano, and voice and also composed a ballet.

Alexander Richter was the head of the music department at the New York High School of Music and Art and on April 30, 1937, invited Petrides to attend rehearsals and conduct the group, understanding the need for female role models for his young students.

| News, Facts, Activities | # WOMEN IN MUSIC | Orchestras; Conductors |

Vol. V. No. 2   *Edited by Frederique Petrides*   December, 1939

It is a pleasure indeed to learn that there is one person alive, and not a man at that, who, far from being awed by Toscanini, dares instead to argue with him about the technique of conducting!! This unusual soul is none else but Sonia, the Maestro's five-year-old , musical granddaughter. According to *Life*, which in its issue for November 27, ran a series of photos on her, the young lady sees no reason why one should use both hands while conducting. Her theory is that one hand is enough and the cameraman snapped her as she was explaining this to the Maestro! Another photo shows her with a switch for a baton as she "takes a lesson in orchestra conducting from her famous grandfather."

How would you caption this paragraph? Out in Chicago, the Women's Symphony pats itself on the back, so to speak, for having a man, Mr. Izler Solomon, as its regular conductor now. Mr. Solomon happens to be the first male to be placed in full command of that group since the days of Conductor Richard Czerwonsky back in 1928. Coincidentally, in far away Los Angeles, the members and friends of the local Women's Symphony are also full of hosannas this season, but for quite a different reason. For the first time in its forty-sixth year, their organization has gone 100 per cent feminine by electing to have a woman as its conductor this season. The new baton wielder is Ruth Haroldson.

The American work on the Orchestrette's program for January 8, at the Carnegie Chamber Music Hall will be Griffes' *Three Tone Pictures;* the violin soloist in Mozart's *Concerto in A Major* will be Frances Shapiro, who like Hinda Barnett, the group's concertmaster, is a Persinger product. As for Frederique Petrides, she will be, "as usual, the conductor", to use a seemingly pet expression of a New York Music critic.

Tickets for concerts make ideal Christmas gifts!

Months ago, when only news of peace and Sibelius came out of Finland, *Musical America* reported on the initial activities of a women's orchestra in Helsinki. The group was founded last year by its conductor, Heidi Sundblad-Halme, who is also a composer, and made its "not inauspicious" debut after rehearsing for about a year.

Lest You Forget!

In their struggle to build a musical career for themselves, "women as a group, and Negroes, have not only the problems of all other musicians, but the additional trials attendant upon the accident of birth," so writes Mr. Howard Taubman, music editor of *The New York Times,* in his recently published book *Music as a Profession* (Scribner's $2.50).

According to a passage in Mr. Taubman's new book: "The only field in music where women stand on an equal footing with men is in singing. . . In other fields the way is harder. . . There have been, and there are now, first rank musicians among the women, and some of them have held their own as box-office draws. But good as they are, the best women instrumental recitalists do not receive fees anywhere as large as the topnotch men.

"The explanation is to be found in custom and prejudice. The public has not yet overcome its feeling that a good female artist, like a good female tennis player, is not in the same class with a good male artist. There is little basis for this feeling. Women are capable of playing as well as men, and some play better. But the female pianists, fiddlers, 'cellists and conductors will have to get the chance to prove it.

. . ."In some major orchestras no women are employed. Several have a female harpist or two. Women have jobs in WPA orchestras and a few are employed regularly on radio house staffs. Otherwise, women must rely on odd jobs, at receptions, luncheons, teas. In England there seems to be more open-mindedness toward women; the British Broadcasting Corporation has eighteen female players in its ranks, or almost one-fifth of the orchestra. . ."

In her well-documented talk before the Music Clubs' Convention on April 26, 1937, Madame Olga Samaroff challenged the Federation to give and help establish equal opportunities in fees and engagements between male and female solo instrumentalists, orchestral players and conductors. Her speech was received most enthusiastically by those who heard it and was printed, a few months later, in the Federation's impressive *Bulletin.* But, now the question arises: has the august Federation done anything with reference to Madame Samaroff's fair-minded plea and recommendations?

Blame it on an association of ideas, if the item in this issue on Toscanini's grandchild brings to mind a seven-year-old American girl, who must be mentioned here, simply for the record, as the first of her age and sex to have led a professional orchestra. The maestrina was Doris Ryan, who, back in 1913, bossed it over thirty-five musicians in parts of a concert at Chicago's Orchestra Hall. Now frowning, or stamping her foot in bursts of temperamental irritation; at other times cutting the air with angry strokes, or shouting commands at the men, the child musician "directed the orchestra in a way that left no doubt in the minds of musicians or audience that she knew exactly what she wished done."

You know of course that one of the traditional arguments advanced against the inclusion of women in orchestras is that the "poor, fair and frail" ones cannot be expected or depended upon to withstand the strain of a tour. Well! At the recent tour of the great Philharmonic Symphony of New York, six of its musicians evidently found the lark beyond their physical endurance and health. Result: they were taken ill and, in consequence, were sent back to their homes and doctors in New York before the completion of the tour. Naturally, this incident is not held against Adam. Imagine, though, the talk, the jokes and the jibes if a casualty like this were to happen to a women's orchestra!

We lament the passing away of Caroline B. Nichols, who many years ago, was nationally known as the founder-conductor of the Fadette Women's Orchestra. She died in Boston on August 16, at the age of seventy-five. Mrs. Nichols started her group in Boston in 1888, naming it after the cheer-spreading heroine in George Sand's novel *La Petite Fadette.* Her venture was active up to 1920 and had to its credit no less than six thousand and sixty-three concerts in Lyceum courses in the United States and Canada, in concert halls, parks, summer resorts and also in first class vaudeville houses.

From a letter to the editor by Mr. A. Richter, Head of the Music Department of New York's High School of Music and Art: "I am in sympathy with women conductors, in so far as they will eventually introduce women into the regular symphony orchestras in our country. In other words, I am as much opposed to 'women orchestras' as I am to 'men orchestras'."

Published by the "Orchestrette Classique", 190 East End Ave., New York City.

VOL. V, NO. 3, FEBRUARY 1940

Erika Morini was born in Vienna, Austria, in 1904 and made her American debut at Carnegie Hall in 1921. In 1943 she became an American citizen. She began her studies with her father, who was the director of the Vienna Conservatory.

Morini was the recipient of Maud Powell's Guadagnini violin. Powell died on tour in 1920 at the age of fifty-one and had bequeathed her instrument to "the next great woman violinist." It was presented a year later to Morini on the occasion of her Carnegie Hall debut. Powell's Guadagnini proved "too big for her hands," and she eventually became the owner of the renowned "Davidoff" Stradivarius (Ammer, 41–42; Clipping Files, NYPL).

Amy Marcy (Cheney) Beach was born in New Hampshire in 1867 and died in New York in 1944. She was one of the first American women to succeed as a composer. Her works were known and performed during her lifetime. Among her many accomplishments, she served as president of the Music Teachers National Association and the Music Educators National Conference, and was co-founder and president of the Association of American Women Composers. She composed both instrumental and vocal works. Her Symphony in E-Minor, op. 32, was the first symphony to be composed by an American woman. The Boston Symphony Orchestra programmed the work in 1896. She was commissioned to write *Festival Jubilate* for the Women's Building at the Chicago World's Fair in 1892. Beach made a major contribution to ornithological science by transcribing bird calls into musical form. Her style was late romantic and for some time was considered "old-fashioned," but her works recently have returned to the concert stage and recordings.

Elsa Hilger, the first woman to become a member of a major American symphony orchestra, was born April 13, 1904, in Vienna. She and her two sisters, a violinist and a pianist, studied at the Vienna Conservatory and toured as a trio. Hilger made her solo debut with the Vienna Philharmonic in 1916 at the age of twelve. In 1920 the Hilger family moved to the United States to begin a series of concert tours. In 1935 she gained a position in the Philadelphia Orchestra that was to last until her retirement in 1969. For twenty-five years she served as associate solo cellist, as well as principal cellist several seasons and on tours. Hilger also was featured periodically as concerto soloist with the Philadelphia Orchestra under Eugene Ormandy. She taught at the Philadelphia Musical Academy and Temple University and maintained a private studio.

| News, Facts, Activities | # WOMEN IN MUSIC | Orchestras; Conductors |

Vol. V. No. 3   *Edited by Frederique Petrides*   February, 1940

Erika Morini is characteristically resentful of being identified as "the greatest woman violinist." Last month Kathleen McLaughlin quoted her, as follows, in the Women's Page of the Sunday *New York Times*. '"What does it matter whether I am a woman or a man'?" Miss Morini demands. ' "Of course there have been many more successful men violinists, but either I am a great violinist or I am not. It means nothing to me to be the greatest woman violinist'."

Orchestras of women players are nothing new in the history of Boston, where a recently launched ensemble —the Women's Symphony Society of Boston—has, as its motto, these words from Chaucer: "I am a wooman, needes most I speake, Or elles swelle til myn herte breke." The program with which this group made its debut last month included the work of a woman composer. Two other women composers,—Mrs. H. H. A. Beach is one of them,—will be represented in the two of the remaining three concerts. There are seventy-seven players in the group. Their conductor is Mr. Alexander Thiede.

"In the hearts of ambitious women the world over there is a special place for the Philadelphia Orchestra (and Leopold Stokowski),"—thus an item in the *N. Y. Times'* Music Section. "For years Mr. Stokowski proclaimed his belief in the ability of the ladies to take their places competently in symphony orchestras, and on several instances he has shown the world that he means what he says. Today the Philadelphia Orchestra has four lady members— a violinist, a 'cellist and two harpists"—and now it "confirms its confidence in the sex" by choosing Elsa Hilger, its woman cellist, "to occupy the first stand" in its Robin Hood Dell series in the summer.

Sixteen boy sopranos will participate in the concert of the Orchestrette Classique, Frederique Petrides, conductor, on Monday evening, March 11, at the Carnegie Chamber Hall. They are from the Choir of *The Church of the Blessed Sacrament,* of which Mr. William A. Foley is the organist and musical director. The boy sopranos will sing the chorale of a little-known short *Mass in E Minor* by Nicolaus Bach. The solo parts will be rendered by Margot Rebeil, soprano; Madeline Reed, contralto; Frederick Schweppe, tenor, and William Fariss, basso.

Tracing the Origin

"The principal reason why we have so few women orchestral musicians is, I think, the simple one that so few of them play wind instruments. They don't play well enough because they haven't had the proper training; and the reason for that lies in the history of orchestral music in the United States," says Mr. Deems Taylor in the course of his new book *The Well-Tempered Listener*. (Simon and Schuster, $2.50.)

As proof for his argument Mr. Taylor says: "Less than half a century ago in this country it was virtually impossible for a would-be orchestral player to get any instruction worthy of the name, on a wind instrument. Even our string players were studying, not for the orchestra, but for the concert platform. In consequence, a majority of the string players in our orchestras, and practically all the members of the brass and woodwind sections, were imported from Continental Europe, from France, Italy, Germany and Russia. Now these men brought with them the Continental attitude toward women, which was that a woman's proper spheres were social and domestic, never professional or political. Such a thing as a woman orchestra player was a monster of which they never could have dreamed.

"Playing orchestral instruments, on the Continent, is not only a strictly masculine occupation, but also, to a striking degree, a hereditary one. You will find famous European families of bassoon players, clarinetists, or oboists. These early, imported musicians of ours taught their sons to play the family instrument; and you will find the sons of many of these men in our orchestras today. Their sons; but never their daughters. If they had any other pupils, those pupils were boys, not girls. And to this day, while American women vote, hold public office, and practice all the professions without shocking our sensibilities, in this particular field, the orchestra, our attitude toward women still remains, I think, rather a Continental one . . .

"However, that prejudice is rapidly crumbling, and is likely to disappear entirely in a few years. For this we have to thank our high-school bands and orchestras, which offer instruction and experience in playing all orchestral instruments to boys and girls alike."

The author of *Music as a Profession* and *Scribner's and Sons,* his publishers, must forgive us for reprinting this irresistible item without their permission: The board of directors of a major orchestra met once to consider the choice of a new conductor. One of the ladies said, 'Let us think. In recent years we have had a German, a Frenchman, an Italian, a Russian and a Dutchman. Isn't it time to look for a conductor in Czecho-Slovakia'?"

Until quite recently, *Women in Music* was under the impression that the great Teresa Carreño was the only woman to have conducted grand opera in times of emergency. (See issue of July, 1938). Thanks, however, to data submitted by Miss Kyveli Aliki, a prominent young actress from Athens, Greece, it is shown that around the time when Carreño was wielding the baton in Carácas, Venezuela, a Miss Elpis Lampelet, was also working in Smyrna, Asia Minor, as emergency conductor for a touring Opera Company. Lampelet was a Greek. For three months in the spring of 1889, she filled successfully the place of the company's maestro, who had resigned without a moment's notice, due to personal differences with some of the singers. And the contributor, who is at present visiting in this country, adds that her data is from the *History of Modern Greek Music* by Synadinos.

"I hope that you will continue sending me *Women in Music* as it is invaluable to me," writes Mrs. Henry S. Drinker, Jr., from Merion, Penna.

"Leginska, why will you not conduct one of our great orchestras?" asked imploringly, a few weeks ago, a writer in a California music magazine. Doesn't the gentleman know that according to Emily Post one must be invited before going to a party?

Paradoxically enough, for a group, which in these days of surrealism has elected to identify itself strictly with classic music, the Orchestrette is always happy to do its share by the moderns. Thus, its next program includes two new compositions: the first performance of Johan Franco's *Serenade Concertante for Piano and Chamber Orchestra,* with William Masselos as the piano soloist; also, a repeat performance of a composition by one of its members, Julia Smith's *Episodic Suite,* which the Orchestrette was the first to introduce in April, 1937.

Published by the "Orchestrette Classique", 190 East End Ave., New York City.

After her retirement, she and her husband, Dr. Willem Ezerman, moved to Middlebury, Vermont, where she has maintained an active recital schedule with her accompanist Catherine Baird (b. January 22, 1944). In 1985 on Hilger's eighty-first birthday, they recorded *Elsa Hilger, First Lady of the Cello* (Clipping Files, NYPL; Vermont Recital Associates).

Hilger is featured as cello soloist in a recent re-release on compact disc of the Brahms Second Piano Concerto, with Rudolf Serkin, pianist, and Eugene Ormandy, conductor, on the Sony Classical (CBS Masterworks) label.

Deems Taylor was born in New York in 1885 and died there in 1966. He was a well-known American composer and critic.

This small paragraph reveals little about the importance of **Sophie Hutchinson Drinker,** who was born in Philadelphia, Pennsylvania, in 1888 and died in Pennsylvania in 1967. She collaborated with her husband, Henry S. Drinker, in writing the catalogue for the **Drinker Library of Choral Music** and organizing the Accademia dei Dilettanti di Musica. In 1932 she formed the Montgomery Singers, an amateur women's chorus. This group was conducted only by women and performed a wide range of both contemporary and standard works. Drinker also wrote articles in the 1930s on women's choruses and the music written for them, which led to her first book, *Music and Women,* published in 1948, a study of women's musical activities from prehistoric times to the twentieth century. Drinker lectured widely about women in music and women's rights, documenting and promoting the activities of women in music. Her papers are housed in the Sophia Smith Collection, Smith College, and the Radcliffe-Schlesinger Collection, Radcliffe College, Harvard University. In her correspondence with Petrides, Drinker often praised Petrides and her work highly.

Elsa Hilger, ca. 1948, Philadelphia.
Photo by Thomas Melvin. Courtesy
Vermont Recital Associates.

Elsa Hilger, 1940, Philadelphia. Photo
by Richard Dooner. Courtesy Vermont
Recital Associates.

VOL. V, NO. 4, APRIL 1940

This eloquently written edition of *Women in Music,* which outlines the need for a systematic survey of outstanding women in all fields of music, was presented to Mary Beard, chairman of archives, the **World Center for Women's Archives, Inc.** In 1940 the address of this group was Rockefeller Center. Petrides had contributed five dollars in June 1938 and a letter acknowledging her membership listed Glenna S. Tinnin as executive secretary; the address was then the Biltmore Hotel, New York. In a letter dated March 7, 1940, Beard discussed Petrides's proposed *Music Project.* Beard asked Mrs. Walter Naumburg of the Naumburg Foundation to condense and organize the music material. Beard commented that no doubt Mrs. Naumburg had asked her husband for help even though she herself was a scientist and enjoyed condensation. Beard also asked whether Petrides would approach Mrs. Astor's secretary for an appointment in order to interest her in their project. (There is a copy of the bylaws of this organization in the Petrides Collection.) In November 1940 Beard wrote Petrides that the organization, which was formed in 1936, had recently polled its members, and the consensus was in favor of dissolving the corporation. The reasons given were the "terrors" of the times, the lack of financial support, and, finally, the impossibility of collecting information from women in other countries. All documents were to be returned with the hope that they would go to local, state, or college libraries. There was, finally, a rather frail expression of hope that the World Center for Women's Archives, Inc., might again be organized when nations were no longer at war.

Orchestrette Concert, April 29.	# WOMEN IN MUSIC	A Special Number

Vol. V. No. 4   *Edited by Frederique Petrides*   April, 1940

Six years ago, the writer of this outline consulted the catalogue files of the New York Public Library for data, historical and contemporary, pertaining to women conductors and women's orchestras. Finding, much to her surprise and chagrin, that the available data were of a decidedly meager and unsatisfactory nature, she decided to undertake a research of her own. Fortunately, her search did not prove fruitless and her published findings on the subject show that the saying "nothing is new under the sun" applies equally well to women in the orchestral field.

Her research in the field of women in the orchestral field showed her that the subject has had its chroniclers here and there in the past. Naturally, these writers were very few and not exactly too generous in their attention to the subject of women in orchestras. The reason why their writings—paragraphs, or mere references in books, short magazine articles, and newspaper stories—were not easily accessible, was due to the fact that they had never been properly assembled and compiled. But the subject was there, a story extending as far back as the days of the ancient Pharaohs. It was merely waiting for some one to lend it form and co-ordination and to present to the public its origin and development.

* * *

From her research on the subject of women in the orchestral field, this writer is of the opinion that the history of Music and Musicians would be considerably enriched if some authoritative organization such as the *World Center of Women's Archives* would undertake a systematic survey of outstanding women in all fields of music as part of its program of "rescuing from oblivion all factual data of unusual women who have made history—a history of their own making, and the common human history they have helped to make."

Naturally, in this undertaking the following subjects should be considered.

a) *Women sponsors of music institutions, music festivals; women patrons of important composers and musicians.*

b) *Women musicologists; women writers on music and musicians; women music critics, lecturers and pedagogues; women directors of institutions such as conservatories, music libraries, etc.*

c) *Women in choral work.*

d) *Pioneer women organizers of musicales; women directors of symphony orchestras and kindred organizations; women's committees for major musical ventures; women managers of concert bureaus; women publicists of music activities.*

e) *Women composers.*

f) *Women as performing artists. Either alone in recital or as soloists with orchestral accompaniment.*

With the possible exception of women composers there is a deplorable lack of available data through which woman's work, past or present, in any of these fields, can be adequately appraised.

* * *

In support of her argument that the undertaking of a factual survey as outlined above would enrich considerably the history of music and the common human history, the writer offers the following reflections:

Women as Sponsors: The cause of

An increasing number of inquiries on various phases of woman's work, past and present, reaches us every month. These inquiries come from men and women in various parts of the country. They show that there is a rising and a wide interest on the subject; also that there is a need for easily available information on it.

This need was recently recognized by the *World Center for Women's Archives*, that excellent and unique organization of which Inez Haynes Irwin is the Chairman; and last month, Mrs. Mary L. Board, the Center's Chairman of Archives, approached the editor of *Women in Music* for a plan of a survey of this hitherto neglected subject.

The report was submitted and approved. It is printed here in its entirety so that interested persons may be informed on the scope of the valuable work which the *World Center for Women's Archives* hopes to be able to undertake in the future on the subject of women in music.—*The Editor.*

---

music is deeply, eternally indebted to those who gave, or who give generously of their time and money to start or to support such institutions as symphony orchestras, chamber orchestras, chamber groups, opera companies, conservatories and schools; to women who gave, or who give generously of their time and money for the support or the launching of music festivals; also, to women whose financial support has made and makes it possible for gifted and unusual composers, instrumentalists and choral leaders to carry on their work.

The contribution of this class of noble-minded women to the cause of music is of inestimable value in terms of culture, of human progress. But how much is known of the great women sponsors and patronesses of the past? Very little, indeed. And how much will their contribution to music, even in our own time, be remembered and appraised, let us say, one hundred years from today?

* * *

Women Musicologists; Women writers of books on music and musicians; women music critics, lecturers and pedagogues; women directors of famous schools of music and music libraries.

Some of the finest books on music and musicians written and published in these days are from the pens of women; some of the most erudite and penetrating articles on music subjects are the brainwork of women. But, contrary to general belief, women are not newcomers in any of these fields. In America, one of the first, if not the first best-selling book on musical topics was written by Amy Fay whose *Music Study in Germany*, was published in 1882. A diligent search of records shows that women have done equally interesting work in kindred lines.

One of the pioneer women music critics in America, Miss May Garretson Evans, is the founder of the Preparatory Department of the Peabody Conservatory of Music in Baltimore, Maryland. While working for the Baltimore *Sun* (on general assignments and occasional music criticism), she was asked by her editor to dig up stories. She complied by writing a piece on her pet idea for a Preparatory Department in the Conservatory. Her story was prominently featured by her paper, and some time later Miss Evans outlined to the Conservatory a detailed plan of her idea. However, since

---

nothing was done with her suggestion, she and her sister opened a school of their own in 1894. The experiment was a great success, and in 1899 their school was merged with the Conservatory as its Preparatory Department. Miss Evans headed it until 1929, when she retired.

* * *

Women Directors of Symphony Orchestras and Kindred Organizations; Women's Committees on Major Musical Ventures; Women Managers of Concert Bureaus, etc.

Before and since the days when Nellie Custis, the adopted daughter of George Washington won for herself the distinction of being the first woman to start giving musicales in this country, women have been most instrumental in spreading music, at first within the confines of their courts or homes, later in their respective communities as amateur organizers and directors of musical activities, and gradually, in a professional capacity. Last year, the Opera House in Helsinki, Finland, was under the direction of a woman director. At present there are women managers of symphonic and chamber orchestras, chamber and choral groups. The number of women concert managers and publicists is also steadily increasing.

* * *

Women Composers: In view of the fact that the subject of women composers has been more generously covered than other subjects within the scope of the proposed survey, it is recommended that women composers be considered only when they are most prominent.

As an illustration of the neglect meted out to distinguished women composers, we have the case of Antonia Bambo, the gifted and prolific composer of the eighteenth century whose name and work are scarcely known to musicians.

Bambo was born in Venice around 1676. She went to France as a young woman and was there awarded a pension by Louis XIV in recognition of her unusual musical talent. Besides a score of songs, she has to her credit a *Te Deum* (for chorus and string orchestra), written sometime before April 1705 in honor of the mother of the Duke of Brittany; a second *Te Deum*, which is of vaster proportions (for chorus and large orchestra); also her masterpiece *Hercules in Love*, which she dedicated to Louis XIV. She also wrote seven psalms called *The Psalms of Penitence.*

An article on this extraordinarily gifted and prolific composer by Yvonne Rosketh, the French musicologist, says: "that compositions forming a whole of such proportions and interest should receive mention by neither the chroniclers, nor the critics, nor the journals of the period, that it should not even be possible to find trace of the pension the King awarded our composer in the registers of the King's accounts (which I have consulted both in the Archives and at the Bibliotheque Nationale of Paris), and that we are totally uninformed of where Antonia passed her old age and of where she died—these are the enigmas of music history."

* * *

The appreciative response of magazine editors, newspaper writers, musicians, students, lecturers, music-lovers and others to the published findings of this writer in the field of women in orchestras, convinces her that a survey such as that proposed in this "tentative plan" would be gratefully received by the community-at-large.

FREDERIQUE PETRIDES,
Conductor, Orchestrette Classique.

Published by the "Orchestrette Classique", 190 East End Ave., New York City.

Orchestrette Concert, October 14.	# WOMEN IN MUSIC	A Short Story Number

Vol. V. No. 5   *Edited by Frederique Petrides*   September, 1940

A Critic and His Mail

The Criticism

"Last night Miss Ethel Winchester gave a piano recital in the Town Hall. If not equally successful in everything she undertook, Miss Winchester at any rate showed that she is a young player of some promise. Like many young people of the present day, she has a technique so remarkable as to make one wonder how she has managed to acquire it in so short a time. It would be unfair to so young a pianist to expect from her an equal ripeness of understanding or feeling; one can only hope that the intelligence she certainly exhibited in one or two of her pieces will develop as she grows older. Some of the music she undertook was evidently more within the scope of her purely pianistic powers than of her spiritual comprehension; it may be doubted, indeed, whether such work as the great Hammerklavier sonata of Beethoven (Op. 106) is not beyond the understanding of any performer of Miss Winchester's years. It says much for her courage that she attempted it; it would perhaps have been an even greater tribute to her wisdom had she resisted the temptation.

In the works the intellectual message of which lay nearer the surface of the notes such as the *Spring Song* of Mendelssohn and the *Marche Militaire* of Schubert-Tausig, Miss Winchester did very well indeed. Some Scarlatti and Couperin pieces were given with considerable charm. In the F sharp Impromptu of Chopin, however, she was perilously near coming to grief. Her memory failed her, and though an impartial listener could not help admiring the never-say-die spirit that carried her through to an end without an actual stoppage, he might still be permitted to doubt whether the notes of her own ingenious invention were quite as good as those that Chopin hit upon. Apparently, the trouble came from insufficient practice of the work. Miss Winchester should take a leaf from the book of the after-dinner speaker and carefully prepare her impromptus. E. N.''

* * *

I. The Letters

"DEAR SIR,—I wonder how you can have the heart—or shall I say the cheek?—to write about any young and deserving musician the way you have written about Miss Winchester: but I notice that you are always brutal towards young people. If I had a nature like yours I should be sorry for myself. I suppose your liver was worse than ever on Tuesday night. I may add that I do not know the concert-giver personally, and was not at the recital in question but my sense of justice moves me to send you this protest.

'FIAT JUSTITIA!'

II. An Anonymous Postcard

"I suppose the young lady you slated yesterday is not a personal friend of yours. If she had been one of those 'comely contraltos' who 'pressed your hand,' you couldn't have found words to express your admiration for her."

III

"Dear Sir:—Why are you always so **hard** on pianists? I notice that you never

Excepting the inclusion of twenty women instrumentalists in Mr. Stokowski's All-American Youth Orchestra, there is no vital news this month on women conductors and orchestras. But, rather than omit this number, we are cordially inviting you to read a short story showing what a London music critic went through because of a review he wrote about an imaginary concert by a woman pianist.

The Londoner is the famous Mr. Ernest Newman, whose book "A Musical Motley", published quite a few years ago, includes the amusing and withal provocative tale which is reprinted here, not only as a sample of what a music critic probably goes through at times, but, also as a sample of what a class of women musicians had to go through—as fiction characters—so that a music critic could conveniently drive home his point.

have a good word for any of them. Surely a good pianist is as admirable as a good singer or violinist? In my opinion Miss Winchester bids fair to be one of the finest pianists in England. I am proud to sign myself

'HER TEACHER.' "

IV

"SIR,—Is it not time that you gave some poor woman a chance? If a male pianist had played as divinely as Miss Winchester did on Tuesday, you would have grovelled at his feet; but because she is a girl you can do nothing but pour out your horrible masculine venom upon the poor shrinking creature. For me her playing, so thrilling, so very truly womanly, was a symbol of the great spiritual work that we women have been called to do in the world—a world at present dominated, but not for much longer, by you soulless brutes of men. Music, the refining art *par excellence* is *our* art, not yours. You men look at it through the purblind eyes of the intellect; to us women it is the purest language of the heart. That is why a man is *incapable* of criticising a true woman's playing; he is like some one listening to the unfolding of *a great* and *holy mystery* in a language he does not understand. If Miss Winchester were of *my* mind she would horsewhip you publicly. In utter contempt *for you and all your sex*,

'TABITHA CATT.' "

V

"DEAR SIR,—I feel I must write and thank you in the name of true art, for the sound and well-deserved trouncing you gave to the presumptuous young person who bored us all at the Town Hall the other evening—a trouncing none the less effective, for those who could read between the lines, for the polite sarcasm in which it was conveyed. The only criticism I would venture to make upon *your* criticism was that it was far too lenient. The young lady's vaulting ambition indeed overleapt itself; in my opinion she ought to give up music and take to typewriting or fancy needlework. I did so sympathize with you

A Critic and His Mail

at having to listen for an hour and a half to such an exhibition of incompetence. I have not the pleasure of knowing you personally, dear sir; but I read with the greatest delight and profit every word that you write and of course I know you well by sight. I could see from your face that you were boiling with rage and disgust, though of course the ordinary person would not have noticed it. I often wonder how you can be as patient as you are with some of the wretched performers you have to listen to.

"May I add that I am giving a piano recital of my own on the 31st, at which I am playing several pieces that were so murdered the other evening? I hope you will honour me with your presence, even if it is only to point out my faults, of which none could be more conscious than myself, though I trust you will find something in my poor efforts to approve of.—With gratitude, Yours Sincerely,

ELIZABETH TOO GOOD

VI

"DEAR MR. NEWMAN—I have just read your notice of my concert and I feel I must write you and thank you before I eat a morsel of breakfast. All night I never got a wink of sleep for thinking what an ass I made of myself at the recital. I made up my mind I would lock the piano in the morning and lose the key. Your article, though I know it to be *too* kind, has quite bucked me up again. It is a relief to me to find you don't think me such a hopeless fool as I thought myself. You were right about the Impromptu. My hat! I never went through such a time as when I felt my memory had side-slipped. What on earth I *did* play after that I don't know. I only hope Chopin wasn't listening to it in whatever place he has gone to.

But I felt dreadfully queer all the evening. As soon as I walked on the platform whom should I see but Jack sitting with that putty-faced May Mortimer. What on earth he can see in that insipid, tow-headed thing I don't know; but anyhow there they were, and I felt she was sneering at me all the time. Then I somehow or other managed to shake a hairpin loose in the Beethoven sonata—I shall remember the very bar to my dying day!—and it settled in the small of my back, and every time I lifted my shoulder blades for a good whack at the keys it just gave me beans. It all seems quite funny now, but Lord! what I went through at the time! Anyhow I am encouraged to think that you really see *some* good in me after all. I won't chuck the piano key away just yet. I'll work hard and try to do better.

"Yes, thanks; mother and I will look in on you at tea-time to-morrow and we'll have some bridge afterwards. Thank heaven there's *something* I can score over you at.—Yours ever gratefully,

ETHEL WINCHESTER."

* * *

(A postscript by Mr. Newman reads as follows: "A number of good people seem to have taken all of this quite seriously. I received several anonymous letters on the subject, abusing me or sympathizing with me." E. N.)

Published by the "Orchestrette Classique", 190 East End Ave., New York City.

| Orchestrette Concert, Dec. 10. | WOMEN IN MUSIC | Give Concert Tickets for Xmas |

Vol. VI No. 1 *Edited by Frederique Petrides* December, 1940

About Ourselves

The history of music activities in New York shows that so far no women's orchestra in the world's biggest musical center has been blessed with a long lease of life. Since those September days in 1871 when the Vienna Ladies' Orchestra started giving its concerts at the Old Steinway Hall on Fourteenth Street, the local musical market has had its share of female intrumental ensembles. However, only one of these groups lasted for about ten years. This was the Women's String Orchestra, which was formed in 1896 and disbanded around 1906. Unlike it, many of the kindred groups which were formed subsequently were comparatively short-lived ventures, lasting one, two, three or five seasons at the most. In view of this, the Orchestrette, which is now at the first stages of its eighth season, may well consider itself lucky.

A group of young players and their conductor, brought together without benefit of publicity, manager, sponsors, etc., held their first rehearsal in 1933 and this is how the Orchestrette was started.

Nowadays, one blushes at the mere thought of how the group's work must have sounded at its first rehearsal and in many other rehearsals during its earlier stages. Fortunately, the venture has almost always attracted to its ranks players with a real love and respect for their profession. And so, if to-day the Orchestrette is a healthy and respected organization, this fact is considerably due to the caliber of its players. Their individual and collective spirit, their respect for the musical aims of their organization show for once more that Mr. Stokowsky was correct when he said in 1916 that: "the particular spirit which women put into music, their kind of enthusiasm, their devotion to anything they undertake would be invaluable in the formation of symphony orchestras."

A handful of concerts a season does not make a livelihood . . . and yet, year after year one sees but few changes in the ranks of the ensemble.

Although predominantly feminine in membership, the Orchestrette has never cared to assume and profess that it is here to show what women can do in orchestras, or, that it has a special mission, the mission of helping female instrumentalists get their deserved recognition in the orchestral world. Its approach to the public has always been the approach of a musical unit striving to gain the respect of discerning music-lovers on the merits of its work and not on the strength of any other consideration.

Deviating at this point, one remembers that shortly after Señor

From The Record

(The following facts are samples of the many little-known historical items printed in *Women in Music*.)

1661.—Samuel Pepys records in his Diary this interesting item: "We went and eat and heard musique at the Globe and saw the simple notion that there is of a woman with a rod in her hands keeping time to the musique while it plays, which is simple methinks."

* * *

1774.—Dr. Charles Burney hears the *Mendicanti* Orchestra in Venice, Italy, and writes: "It was really curious to see, as well as to hear every part of this excellent concert performed by females, violins, tenors, bases, harpsichordists and double bases..."

* * *

1880.—Sidney Lanier, *Poet Laureate of the South*, says in an article published in *Scribner's*: "...Let our young ladies—always saving of course those who have a gift for the piano—leave that and address themselves to the violin, the flute, the oboe, the harp, the clarinet, the bassoon, the kettledrum. It is more than possible that upon some of these instruments the superior daintiness of the female tissue might finally make the woman a more successful player than the man..."

* * *

1888.—Caroline B. Nichols forms in Boston, Mass., the Fadette Women's Orchestra. She doesn't know, of course, that her group is destined to enjoy a most active and profitable life up to 1920.

___

Iturbi was reported in 1937 as having said that women "cannot achieve greatness in music", a trade magazine recommended editorially that the Orchestrette should play a program devoted exclusively to works by women composers.

That suggestion was not followed and for a very good reason. It is bad enough to have orchestras composed of women or of men only, instead of having mixed orchestras all over the land. It is worse to draw a dividing line between works by male or female composers — and this holds true for creative work in every branch of the arts, in painting, sculpture, poetry and the dance.

It is no secret, of course, that a precarious financial status has always threatened the ensemble. This condition plus the tenacity with which the Orchestrette has survived thus far, caused someone to remark that the ensemble is like a "deserving but neglected stepchild in the orchestral world of New York." The characterization is not incompatible with the facts of the case.

About Ourselves

But the "stepchild" feels it is entitled to be proud of itself, its record.

It has never compromised in the matter of arranging its programs.

It has never played politics in its selection of works by contemporary composers.

Its choice of music and the character of its performances have always been guided by a high regard for the taste and the intelligence of the public.

And it has never succumbed to the indiscriminate vogue for "first performarnce", since this much abused line underneath a composition often really only means "first and last performance."

___

Another source of gratification to the Orchestrette is the educational work undertaken and carried consistently through *Women in Music*, its own publication.

Women in Music was started in the summer of 1935 for the purpose of acquainting its readers with little-known historical facts pertaining to women conductors, instrumentalists and orchetras, and, with current developments in this special field. It is sent free of charge to newspaper and magazine editors, to libraries, music schools, institutions and to individuals in New York and elsewhere. It is the first and only publication of its kind in the history of music journalism. Its circulation averages about 2500 copies per issue.

Has the publication succeeded in attracting the attention of the public to the field which it has attempted to cover? Who knows! Nevertheless, let it be remarked here that its subject matter has often found its way into the columns of many newspapers and magazines from coast to coast.

Excluding the various music or general magazines in New York and elsewhere which have quoted from *Women in Music*, here is a partial list of newspapers which have used or quoted subjet matter from the same source: *New York Times*; *New York Sun*; *New York World-Telegram*; *New York Daily News*; *New York Post*; *Baltimore Sun*; *Chicago Tribune*; *San Diego Union*; *Los Angeles Times*; *Long Beach (California) Press Telegram*; the *Philadelphia Inquirer* and those publications which use its syndicated *Everybody's Weekly*.

___

It would be a pity, if through lack of the necesary support the Orchestrette would eventually find itself compelled to suspend its activities.

With the above in mind the undersigned hopes that influential and understanding music-lovers will finally elect to take the initiative of forming a committee for the worthy purpose of enabling her group to continue its activities for many seasons to come.

Frederique Petrides

Published by the "Orchestrette Classique", 100 East End Ave., New York City.

Hudson Valley Symphony Orchestra

Frederique Petrides, Conductor

Appendix: *"Outline of a Prejudice"*

by Frédérique Joanne Petrides

Friends and apologists of women in music must have been temporarily taken aback in 1892, the year when the American translation of Anton Rubinstein's "A Conversation on Music" appeared in New York. In the course of this book, the great pianist sneered at woman's ability and accomplishments in the creative and the interpretative spheres of music. He also read in the increase of women as instrumental players or composers the signs of the downfall of music.

Rubinstein was neither the first nor the last to sound the tocsin on the subject of women in music. Around 1880, Otto Gumprecht, a typical champion of the *status quo* regarding barriers existing against women musicians, was uttering loud protest in Berlin against the candidacy *en masse* of the fair sex for virtuosoships. According to the mournful Teuton such candidacies were characteristic of the "morbid symptons of the age."

Even Shakespeare does not sound as if he had much, if any, respect for feminine musical ability. His words: "Will my daughter prove a good musician? I think she'll sooner prove a good soldier," typify in part a widespread prejudice which lasted for centuries. As long as that prejudice reigned unchallenged, women were prevented from acquiring a serious musical education. They also were being discouraged from venturing outside the operatic field for musical careers.

Since the days of Palestrina and up to the middle of the nineteenth century woman was taught music as a pastime and then only in its most elementary forms. Her musical education seldom advanced beyond playing the

The article "Outline of a Prejudice" first appeared in the *Pacific Coast Musician,* October 19, 1935.

lute, the harpsichord, the clavichord, the virginal and finally the pianoforte.

On the practical career side, the musically gifted and at the same time daring and unconventional female was allowed to seek self-expression as a singer only about A.D. 1600, the period when the opera was introduced in Europe. But, women who had ambitions for a serious study of music or who aspired for a career as composers or instrumentalists were more or less pitied, when not denounced, as the victims of some mental aberration. With few exceptions, those of the sex who, urged by genius or irrepressible talent, now and then would emerge as composers or instrumental players, were doing so at their own risk. Social laws and prejudice were against them. For instance:

As late as the eighties, to be told that a composition was the work of a woman was the equivalent of its condemnation beforehand. This compelled many women to use masculine pen names in order to have their works published. After the gifted Fanny Mendelssohn (1805–1847) had been dissuaded by her famous brother from publishing her works on account of her sex, she had some of her compositions appear as his own in his "Songs Without Words." Anxious to get a musical degree, Elizabeth Stirling, the English composer and organist, submitted in 1856 to Oxford her beautiful CXXX Psalms for Five Voices and Orchestra. Her work was accepted and praised. But the degree was denied her "for want of power to confer same upon a woman."

The history of professional women players between 1700 and 1850, shows that the class was often censored for bad taste and affrontery for having chosen the piano, the violin, the 'cello, the clarinet and other kindred instruments. "Our modern belles are determined not to be excluded from exercising any department of art; all we now want is a female virtuoso on the bassoon and trombone and we believe the list will then be complete." Thus read the sarcastic comment of a Munich critic in 1823, *a-propos* of a concert given in that city by the celebrated clarinetist, Mme. Krahmer.

The critics were full of hosannahs regarding the genius and accomplishments of Signora Parravicini, the great Italian violinist who was born in Turin in 1769. But they objected to her instrument. They thought that the violin was "not suited to a female, a fact universally admitted and which no skill or address can get over with."

Sometime before 1774, Schmelling, the German child prodigy who later became famous as the singer Mara, gave a number of recitals in London.

Immediately, various undoubtedly socially correct English ladies persuaded her to give up her instrument. The ladies "disliked female fiddlers," an attitude which impelled a contemporary critic living years ahead of his time to write: "We cannot but regard the exclusion of females from the violin as a prejudice and nothing but a prejudice."

There is little doubt that Mozart must have felt a keen repulsion at this and other kindred discriminations of his time against female musicians when he declared that women have more natural gift for stringed instruments than males, a gift which he attributed to their greater delicacy of touch and also to a readier access of a conductor to their emotions.

The prejudice against a serious musical education or careers for women in music has kept waning increasingly since 1850. In 1876, the English High School of London began admitting for the first time women students for the violin. Germany already had admitted a woman as a Royal Professor in the Dresden School of Music. Between 1880 and 1882 the Mendelssohn Scholarship in England went to a member of the fair sex. Women were now admitted at the Royal Academy and the Royal College. They also could enter the Cambridge examination for musical degrees, an event which opened the doors of more colleges and conservatories for them.

The isolated class of people who from the very beginning had been favorably disposed toward women in music had gained a good number of converts to their viewpoint since the dawn of the nineteenth century. The eighties saw this element upholding with fervor and even militancy the principle that woman's musical genius and talents would develop in exact proportion to the advantages for education and practical careers at her command. Naturally, those on the other side of the fence neither could digest nor accept meekly this principle. In the meantime, the class of women who were winning regional or international fame as concert artists, and to a lesser extent as music teachers, was consistently growing stronger and more impressive in Europe.

These developments exercised their practical influence in the New World. Gradually the piano ceased being the instrument *par excellence* for the American girl. Between 1892 and 1900 the increase of women actively engaged as music students, teachers or concert players under the American sky demonstrated the fact that our women were quick to appreciate their recently unfolded rights for equal educational and professional advantages in the musical world.

Freed from the shackles and tatters of the old tradition and prejudice, American and European women in music are now universally hailed as important factors in the concert and teaching fields and as promising and at the same time fast developing assets in the creative spheres of the profession. Their development during the last thirty years in all branches of music has already disproved the unfair prejudice expounded even by Shakespeare. Furthermore, their record in the profession proves that the signs which, according to Rubinstein, indicated the downfall of music, were in reality signs of a fuller, a more abundant and representative musical life for both sexes.

Works Cited

Ammer, Christine. *Unsung: A History of Women in American Music.* Westport, Conn.: Greenwood Press, 1980.

Anderson, Bonnie S., and Judith P. Pinsser. *A History of Their Own: Women in Europe from Prehistory to the Present,* vol. 1. New York: Harper & Row, 1988.

Baker, Theodore. *Baker's Biographical Dictionary of Musicians,* 7th ed. Rev. by Nicolas Slonimsky. New York: Schirmer Books, 1984.

Brown, James D., and Stephen S. Stratton. *British Musical Biography: A Dictionary of Musical Artists, Authors, and Composers Born in Britain and Its Colonies.* London: William Reeves, 1897.

Cohen, Aaron I. *International Encyclopedia of Women Composers.* 2 vols. 2nd ed. New York: Books & Music (USA) Inc., 1987.

Hitchcock, H. Wiley, and Stanley Sadie, eds. *The New Grove Dictionary of American Music.* 4 vols. London: MacMillan Press Ltd., 1986.

Hixon, Donald L., and Don Hennessee. *Women in Music: A Bibliography.* Metuchen, N.J.: Scarecrow Press, 1975.

Holmes, John L. *Conductors on Record.* Westport, Conn.: Greenwood Press, 1982.

LePage, Jane Weiner. *Women Composers, Conductors, and Musicians of the Twentieth Century: Selected Biographies,* vol. 2. Metuchen, N.J.: Scarecrow Press, Inc., 1983.

McCarthy, S. Margaret W. "Amy Fay: Progress of a Biography." Abstract and Paper. Third Annual Women in Music Symposium, State University of New York at Buffalo. October 1989.

McGillen, Geoffrey, and Mary Shannon McGillen. "The Teaching and Artistic Legacy of Olga Samaroff (1880-1948)." Abstract and Paper. Third Annual Women in Music Symposium, State University of New York at Buffalo. October 1989.

Mize, J. T. H. *The International Who Is Who in Music.* 5th ed. Chicago: Sterling Publishing, 1951.

Neuls–Bates, Carol, ed. *Women in Music: An Anthology of Source Readings from the Middle Ages to the Present.* New York: Harper & Row, 1982.

Palmer, Russell. *British Music.* London: Knapp, Drewett & Sons Ltd., 1947.

Pool, Jeannie. "The Women-In-Music Movement, Then and Now." Keynote address for Opus 3: Women in Music Conference, University of Kansas, Lawrence, Kan. In *International League of Women Composers Newsletter.* Spring 1985.

Thompson, Oscar. *The International Cyclopedia of Music and Musicians.* New York: Dodd, Mead & Co., 1964.

Index

Note: references to the reproductions of the *Women in Music* newsletter are indicated by italic page numbers.